APPRAISAL AND STAFF DEVELOPMENT IN SCHOOLS

Jeff Jones

David Fulton Publishers

London

David Fulton Publishers Ltd
2 Barbon Close, London WC1N 3JX

First published in Great Britain by
David Fulton Publishers 1993

British Library Cataloguing in Publication Data

A catalogue record for this book is available from the British Library

ISBN 1-85346-279-9

Printed in Great Britain by Bell and Bain Ltd, Glasgow.

CONTENTS

LIST OF FIGURES

LIST OF EXAMPLES

LIST OF ACTIVITIES

INTRODUCTION

At the end of a school day when children come home from school, the chances are that they will have little or nothing to say about the National Curriculum programmes of study, whether attainment targets have or have not been covered, the arguments for and against grant-maintained status, or the increased responsibilities of governing bodies. What they are likely to talk about are the teachers, their skills, their funny ways, their care and concern, their ability to stimulate and maintain interest, and so on. The reason for this is quite simple. No matter what legislation continues to emanate from central government, the ultimate factor in determining the quality of what goes on in classrooms is the teacher.

The introduction of more systematic approaches to appraisal and professional development recognises the importance of teachers in the crusade to improve the quality of what is taught and learnt in classrooms. Appraisal is part of a continuous process for securing the extension of the professional skills of teachers and the improvement of schools. It does so by addressing teachers' personal fulfilment, and offering a means of helping them take stock of their professional performance, their career hopes and their targets for action.

The School Teacher Appraisal Regulations and Circular 12/91 (School Teacher Appraisal) issued by the DfE in July 1991, made appraisal a requirement for all teachers employed on a regular basis. Now that appraisal is a major aspect of their professional lives, it is to be hoped that teachers will learn to view it as an opportunity as well as an entitlement.

> **Like all innovations, appraisal can either be regarded as an opportunity to be seized or as an imposition to be endured. Unless staff appraisal is seized as an opportunity, by which the organisation and the individual can both benefit, there is a danger that the result will be the imposition of a bureaucratic assessment system which will be inimical to a profession dedicated to development and improvement.**

> **Fidler and Cooper, 1988**

The central theme of this book is the effective management of staff development through appraisal. It has been written in an attempt to help colleagues in schools and in colleges, at whatever level of responsibility, to understand the new national appraisal system introduced by the DfE, to gain maximum benefit from the process and to develop their own appraisal arrangements. The book considers the background to appraisal and its purpose, as well as its importance in enhancing the development of staff and the effectiveness of schools. Furthermore, the layout and content of the book makes it a valuable resource for schools with established schemes to review their current appraisal policy and practice. In doing so it places heavy emphasis on the need to harmonise the personal and professional development of teachers and the needs of the institution.

There seems to be a cautious optimism in schools that appraisal, far from being the crude assessment of standards once feared by teachers, will in fact help bring about the development of professional skills and knowledge.

The author is conscious of the heavy and competing demands currently being made upon staff in schools and colleges. For that reason, within its covers, this book encapsulates all of the basic information required by those teachers intending to implement an appraisal scheme. It offers a balance of factual information, comments, examples and activity. The following features have been included in order that the reader can access the relevant information as easily as possible:

- the text is presented in a clear and concise form without jargon;

- a synopsis of the main factors influencing the demand for appraisal is provided to equip the reader with valuable insight and information;

- extracts are quoted from the Statutory Regulations and Circular 12/91 which are supported by examples;

- examples, drawn from a wide range of sources, have been included to illustrate some of the key points made and to clarify some of the issues raised;

- structured activities are included to enable colleagues to discuss issues and to devise strategies for addressing such issues;

- the relevant section of Circular 12/91 is quoted verbatim within the shaded boxes at the start of each section so that the reader does not have to refer to additional documents.

Dr J L Jones
May 1993

CHAPTER ONE

Appraisal: a context for development

Background

The development of appraisal in schools has had a chequered history. A number of factors have contributed to this situation, not least the inability of policy-makers and educationists to agree on a clear statement of the purpose of appraisal. Confusion also exists over recurring tensions, such as whether appraisal is for professional development or for accountability, and whether the process should be linked to pay and dismissal.

Trends outside education have also influenced thinking on the issue of appraisal and several models from industry and commerce have been available to those in the education service.

Interest in formal teacher appraisal can be traced back to the mid 1970s but it was not until 1983 that the Government, in a move to encourage greater accountability in the education service, stated its belief that:

> ...those responsible for managing the school teacher force have a clear responsibility to establish, in consultation with their teachers, a policy for staff deployment and training based on a systematic assessment of every teacher's performance and related to their policy for the school curriculum.

The White Paper went on to say:

> ...employers can manage their teacher force effectively only if they have accurate knowledge of each teacher's performance. The Government believe that for this purpose formal assessment of teachers' performance is necessary and should be based on classroom visiting by the teachers head or head of department, and an appraisal of pupil's work and of the teachers contribution to the life of the school. They therefore welcome the interest currently shown amongst employers and teacher associations about career development and professional assessment of teachers.

> **Teaching Quality, DES,1983**

This notion was reinforced two years later in another Government White Paper, *Better Schools* (DES,1985). It clearly indicated its intention to introduce appraisal by stating:

> ...that the regular and formal appraisal of the performance of all teachers is necessary if LEAs are to have reliable, comprehensive and up-to-date information necessary for the systematic and effective provision of professional support and development and the deployment of staff to best advantage...Taken together, these decisions should result in improved deployment and distribution of the talent within the teaching force, with all teachers being helped to respond to changing demands and to realise their full professional potential by developing their strengths and improving upon their weaknesses...

> **Better Schools, DES, 1985**

The firm commitment to introduce such regulations was incorporated in the 1986 Education (No 2) Act which stated that the Secretary of State:

> **may by regulations make provision requiring local education authorities, or such other persons as may be prescribed, to secure that the performance of teachers...is regularly appraised.**

> **Education (No 2) Act, 1986**

Throughout, the profession was at great pains to point out that appraisal had always been a feature of the working of British schools, albeit in an ad hoc, unofficial and unstructured way. The appraisal of teachers is not new, therefore, but:

> **What is new is the Government's determination to ensure that the performance of teachers is regularly appraised and to introduce legislation requiring LEAs to implement appraisal.**

> **Fearon, 1986**

However, the major impetus for appraisal came from a rather unusual source - the industrial dispute of the mid-1980s. Reactions from teachers and their associations were generally positive until the issue became enmeshed in the protracted negotiations over pay and conditions. The dispute, which was referred to the Advisory Conciliation and Arbitration Service (ACAS), led to the establishment of a special working party to consider appraisal and professional development.

The 1986 ACAS agreement regarded appraisal as a positive process, designed to help and support teachers. Furthermore, it emphasised the continuity and developmental nature of the process. The report defined appraisal as:

> **...a continuous and systematic process intended to help individual teachers with their professional development and career planning, and to help ensure that the in-service training and deployment of teachers matches the complementary needs of individual teachers and the schools**

> **ACAS, 1986**

The publication of the ACAS working group report (ACAS, 1986) on appraisal and training was a major turning point since it gave rise to the DES-funded School Teacher Appraisal Pilot Study (1987-89), involving six local education authorities - Croydon, Cumbria, Newcastle-upon-Tyne, Salford, Somerset and Suffolk. These pilot schemes demonstrated that appraisal, based on the guidelines incorporated into the ACAS agreement, could benefit both teachers and schools, leading ultimately to improvements in the quality of teaching and learning.

> **Figure 1.1:** **SCHOOL TEACHER APPRAISAL PILOT STUDY (STAPS):**
> **FACTS AND FIGURES**
>
>
> - **Set up following the ACAS Working Group Report 1986**
> - **Overseen by the National Steering Group (NSG)**
> - **Involved 6 LEAs - Croydon, Cumbria, Newcastle, Salford, Somerset, Suffolk**
> - **Involved 1690 teachers and 190 headteachers**
> - **Evaluated by Cambridge Institute of Education**
> - **Final report issued via National Steering Group (NSG) in October 1989**

The National Steering Group, set up to monitor the progress of the pilot authorities, put forward agreed recommendations on a national framework for appraisal (NSG, 1989). The report, compiled on the basis of the six pilot schemes, placed appraisal unequivocally within the context of professional development. The NSG report identified the key principles and procedures which government should prescribe under Section 49 of the Education (No 2) Act 1986. It also indicated what should be contained in any related circular on appraisal. The principles contained in the National Framework are set out below:

Appraisal schemes shall be designed to:

(i) **help teachers to identify ways of enhancing their professional skills and performance,**

(ii) **assist in planning the in-service training and professional development of teachers individually and collectively,**

(iii) **help individual teachers, their head teachers, governing bodies and local education authorities (where appropriate) to see where a new or modified assignment would help the professional development of individual teachers and improve their career prospects,**

(iv) **identify the potential of teachers for career development, with the aim of helping them, where possible, through appropriate in-service training,**

(v) **provide help to teachers having difficulties with their performance, through appropriate guidance, counselling and training,**

(vi) **inform those responsible for providing references for teachers in relation to appointments,**

(vii) **enhance the overall management of schools.**

National Steering Group, 1989

Her Majesty's Inspectors, in their report *Developments in the Appraisal of Teachers* (DES, 1989), also observed that appraisal, if sensibly planned and practised, has much value. They emphasised not only that:

properly resourced and prepared-for appraisal can be an effective element in the management of current educational reform.

but that:

Appraisal has contributed to the better identification of in-service training needs. The

management of staff and the curriculum has improved as a result of better communication and awareness. It has had a marked effect on the performance of individual teachers.

Development in the Appraisal of Teachers; October 1989:HMI

A well planned and effectively managed scheme for appraisal can do much to enhance the professional development of teachers and headteachers and at the same time improve the management of schools. The HMI Report (1989) makes this same point:

> **...it is important that appraisal is not done for its own sake but is seen as a tool integral to the management of other initiatives and strategies.**

HMI Report, 1989

The statutory regulations widely expected to emanate from the NSG proposals were not forthcoming. The then Secretary of State, John MacGregor, responded in September 1990 and deferred the introduction of a national system, preferring instead to leave the decision to individual LEAs, a move described by some as a recipe for inertia.

Meanwhile, the findings and recommendations of both the School Management Task Force and the Interim Advisory Committee Report on Schoolteachers' Pay and Conditions of Service (IAC, 1990) had acknowledged the importance of appraisal. Both had reinforced the growing belief that appraisal had the potential to bring about the development of both institutions and the individuals within them:

> **Every teacher deserves the opportunity for regular review of their professional and career development and we look forward to the rapid introduction of a national system of appraisal as an urgent priority.**

School Management Task Force Report, 1990

> **We are clear that appraisal is a vital tool for managers of schools...we hope that the Secretary of State's consultations will enable rapid progress to be made towards a sensible and practical national scheme...We have sought...to develop a framework for teachers' pay and conditions in which the quality of teaching and learning can be improved. We regard teacher appraisal as an important element in developing and maintaining that improvement.**

IAC: 1991: para.41

Later that year (11.12.90), the new Secretary of State, Kenneth Clarke, declared his intention to introduce regulations requiring LEAs to implement appraisal in the schools maintained by them. The Statutory Regulations and the accompanying Circular (12/91) published in July 1991, which were largely based on the NSG recommendations, identified the main features of the national scheme.

Benefits of appraisal

Appraisal and staff development are central to the whole range of accountability measures that have been introduced since the mid-1980s and are therefore of vital importance in improving performance in the classroom and the status of the profession.

The education service in general and the teaching profession specifically can be legitimately accused of failing to follow the example of other organisations such as the health service, the civil service, the police force, business and commerce in embracing the notion of appraisal. That varying forms of appraisal, albeit informal in their structure, have existed in schools and colleges is not in doubt (Turner & Clift, 1985). The staff in such institutions have involved themselves in regular review, staff development discussion/interviews and visits to colleagues' classrooms. The question that many colleagues therefore ask is, "Why do we need a DES Regulation forcing us to do appraisal?"

The answer is in two parts. First, the supportive scenario highlighted above, whereby staff are involved in appraisal for their professional development, is by no means common in all schools and the entitlement of all colleagues to the opportunity needs to be secured. Second, teachers are entitled to a formal process of performance appraisal which focuses on setting achievable targets in the light of feedback. As Margaret Maden (County Education Officer, Warwickshire) put it:

> ...in a period of intense and rapid change, an appraisal or, more appropriately, a review and development process is urgently needed. Such a process ought to be seen as an entitlement. If teachers are to develop their skills and knowledge in significantly new directions then they ought to be able to sit down once a year at least and, in a systematic way, review their work and agree achievable targets for the following year. This would probably do more than anything else to make the process of change manageable and to raise professional self-esteem, especially if one of the outcomes was a more bespoke approach to staff development and INSET needs.
>
> in: *Education* 20.10.89

Given that the focal point of every educational initiative should be the improvement of childrens learning through a better understanding of their needs, it is reasonable to try to gauge the benefits to the learning process and ultimately to the pupils which are likely to accrue from a scheme of appraisal.

What can appraisal offer the staff?

Staff appraisal concentrates the mind on what's important.

Personnel Manager, Procter & Gamble Ltd

Unless there are genuine benefits from appraisal for the staff of the organisation, there is little point in embarking on the scheme. Staff must feel that they are deriving some benefit from the process, rather than seeing it as a paper exercise or one that is superficial. The extent to which staff gain from the appraisal process will depend, in large measure, on the quality of planning, the extent of the commitment and the rigour with which the scheme is operated and evaluated. In brief, appraisal should offer teachers.

- recognition of effective practice
- greater clarity of role
- improved feedback on performance
- a more open working environment
- better understanding of the requirements of the job

- an opportunity to influence policy
- a more systematic analysis of training and development needs
- greater accuracy of references
- greater awareness of career development factors
- support in work-related issues
- improved job satisfaction.

...people work more effectively when they know what is expected of them...if they know that their performance is being monitored by a boss who is prepared to be honest with them at least once a year, but hopefully much more frequently.

Ron Shepherd, Training Manager, Ford Motor Company

What can appraisal offer the institution?

Although the central concern must be with the personal and professional development of teachers, appraisal has a vital role to play in the overall development of the institution. Schools can derive the following benefits from appraisal:

- more accurate information about teacher performance
- a more purposeful organisation
- clearer lines of responsibility and communication
- an improved management
- a more open ethos and supportive environment
- identification and coordination of staff INSET needs
- a better informed school
- a more accountable organisation
- enrichment of provision for pupils
- increased staff morale.

What can appraisal offer the pupils?

The principal aim of appraisal is to enhance and maximise the educational opportunities of pupils through the professional growth of teachers. Pupils can benefit through

- a clearer understanding by teachers of their needs
- more systematic planning of learning experiences
- a wider variety of learning opportunities
- curriculum content which is more relevant to their needs at various ages and stages of development
- experience of styles of teaching which make learning a more active process.

What can appraisal offer the Local Authority?

With the investment of time and money made by LEAs in taking responsibility for implementing appraisal on behalf of the Government, it is perhaps reasonable for LEAs to ask "What's in it for us?"

- improved quality of educational provision
- more purposeful management of schools
- organisational development of schools
- more accurate information about teacher performance
- improved content of teacher references
- more specific information about INSET requirements
- improved staff development patterns to match needs
- improved staff morale
- a better motivated workforce.

Figure 1.2 illustrates the major influences on the development of appraisal.

Figure 1.2:	THE MAIN POLITICAL FACTORS INFLUENCING THE DEVELOPMENT OF APPRAISAL
1944	Education Act
1972	The Bains Report
1972	The James Report
1974	Assessment of Performance Unit established by DES
1976	The Ruskin College Speech which launched the Great Debate
1976	The Auld Report - public enquiry into the William Tyndale School
1977	The Taylor Committee
1978	Primary Education in England (HMI)
1979	Aspects of Secondary Education (HMI)
1981	The School Curriculum (Circular 6/81)
1981	Practical Curriculum
1983	Teaching Quality
1984	Education Observed 3: Good Teachers
1985	Quality in Schools: Evaluation and Appraisal
1985	Better Schools
1985	Those Having Torches (The Graham Report)
1986	Education (No2) Act
1986	ACAS Working Party
1986	School Teacher Appraisal Pilot Projects
1987	In the Light of Torches (The Graham Report)
1987	School Teachers Pay and Conditions of Employment: The Government Proposals
1988	Education Reform Act
1989	Development in the Appraisal of Teachers (HMI)
1989	National Steering Group Report
1991	Interim Advisory Committee
1991	Statutory Regulations and Circular 12/91

CHAPTER TWO

Appraisal for professional development

If the process of appraisal is to be part of the development of teachers and of schools, it needs also to be part of the pattern of school life, linked to the schools other routines and developmental activities. It needs to be context-based within the legal framework provided by the Department for Education.

A school which is self-managing, self-developing and self-evaluating is likely to be one in which all teachers

- freely exchange ideas
- share concerns
- are used to reflecting upon their own performance
- contribute to discussion
- take part in the process of decision-making
- have individual areas of strength and weakness identified and supported.

The prerequisites of an effective appraisal process can be described in precisely the same terms. Each of the above characteristics is a vital ingredient of an appraisal process which arises from, as well as leads to, the development of teachers and organisations.

However, a list of descriptors does not in itself provide a structure which enables managers to manage the process of appraisal. The management process should ensure that at LEA level and at school level, teacher appraisal is

- **planned** - with identified goals and objectives coupled with realistic resourcing

- **organised** - so that individuals and groups are clear about their roles and responsibilities

- **monitored** - so that plans and organisation may be modified in the light of accumulating experience

- **positive** - so that teachers will want to become involved and derive benefit

- **developmental** - creating opportunities for teachers to build on their experiences.

Appraisal and Staff Development

Appraisal is a natural progression from the staff development and school development planning activities already well established in many schools. Staff and professional development strategies have enabled many schools and teachers to gain the skills and understanding necessary to participate in appraisal. Appraisal is increasingly becoming a major part of the school development process and of the professional development of all teachers.

There are many definitions of staff development but what the various definitions have in common is a recognition that staff development is a planned process which enhances the quality of pupil learning. At the heart of this process is the identification and clarification of the needs of teaching staff within the context of the school as a whole. Staff development should support the individual, as well as a range of groups within the school. Circular 12/91 states that:

appraisal procedures shall in particular aim to-

(a)   recognise the achievements of school teachers and help them to identify ways of improving their skills and performance;

(b)   help school teachers, governing bodies and local education authorities to determine whether a change of duties would help the professional development of school teachers and improve their professional prospects;

(c)   identify the potential of teachers for career development, with the aim of helping them, where possible, through appropriate in-service training;

(d)   help school teachers having difficulties with their performance, through appropriate guidance, counselling and training;

(e)   inform those responsible for providing references for school teachers in relation to appointments;

(f)   improve the management of schools.

Appraisal in the Context of School Development Planning

The principal aim of appraisal is the improvement of teaching and learning. It is a professional development strategy for bringing about individual growth and institutional development. As such, it must progressively feature as an integral part of the schools staff development strategy, interacting with

- the aims and values of the school
- the roles and responsibilities of staff
- the school development plan
- existing good practice
- recruitment, selection and induction procedures
- the professional development and training of staff
- the monitoring and evaluation strategy of the school.

Paragraph 11 of the Circular draws attention to the need for appraisal to be established within the context of wider school development.

CIRCULAR 12/91: APPRAISAL AND SCHOOL DEVELOPMENT PLANS
para.
11   Appraisal should be set in the context of the objectives of the school, which will generally be
       expressed in a school development plan. Appraisal should support development planning and
       vice versa. The schools objectives in a particular year should be linked with appraisal, so that
       for example, professional development targets arising from appraisal may be related to agreed
       targets and tasks in the development plan. Similarly appraisal targets, when taken together,
       should provide an important agenda for action for the school as a whole. Targets set during
       appraisal should therefore meet the needs of the schools as well as those of individual
       appraisees. Setting appraisal within the framework of school development should also ensure
       that targets are realistic and make the best use of available resources.

The interest, in recent years, in school development planning provides a useful strategy for linking appraisal and other complementary review procedures and initiatives together in a practical and coherent way. In order to bring about improvements in the teaching and learning already taking place in schools, it is vital to ensure that appraisal is an integral part of the schools development plan. Such a plan should be an explicit statement of what the school is attempting to achieve, not only in academic terms but in relation to activities covering staff/student development, management of resources, community links, and so on. The plan should establish clear targets for the school to aim for and its contents should be shared with all the agencies that are likely to be able to support its implementation, e.g. staff, governors, parents, LEA, etc.

Publication by the DES in 1990 of the booklet *Planning for School Development* presented schools with a helpful process for prioritising and planning strategically. It suggested that schools go through three stages:

- the justification and creation of a plan
- an understanding that the processes involved in creating and implementing the plan are important
- an understanding that the effective management of those processes is the real key to success.

The introduction of appraisal has a dual implication for school development plans. First, it must be properly planned - with appropriate financing, training, resourcing and time. Second, appraisal must link closely with the development plan. Individual targets must, where appropriate, be part of the corporate plan.

> Two principal aims of appraisal are to facilitate the professional growth of the individual
> teacher and to effect institutional improvement. Essentially, however, appraisal is about the
> judgement of performance. Consequently, one aim might be to use such judgements to
> measure the performance of individual teachers against what is expected of them, and to
> inform decisions about what action is appropriate to meet their needs.
>
> HMI, 1989

In basic terms, the introduction of appraisal will assist with

- setting of whole school targets
- identification of professional development needs
- aggregation of professional development needs to inform the LEA
- highlighting of resource implications
- development of school self-review.

It would seem crucial that staff are involved as much as possible in the discussion of the schools priorities for development prior to their appraisal, and that documents such as the school aims, the development plan and the staff development strategy are made available to them. In this way the appraisal targets identified are likely to be of benefit to the professional development of staff as well the development of the institution.

Figure 2.1 below illustrates the link between appraisal and school improvement as well as the potential benefits of appraisal to both individuals and the institution as a whole. Appraisal should result in staff working more effectively, having a higher level of motivation and enhanced developing professional skills. Furthermore, appraisal enables the institution to make better use of peoples skills, develop their potential and understand their particular role within the establishment.

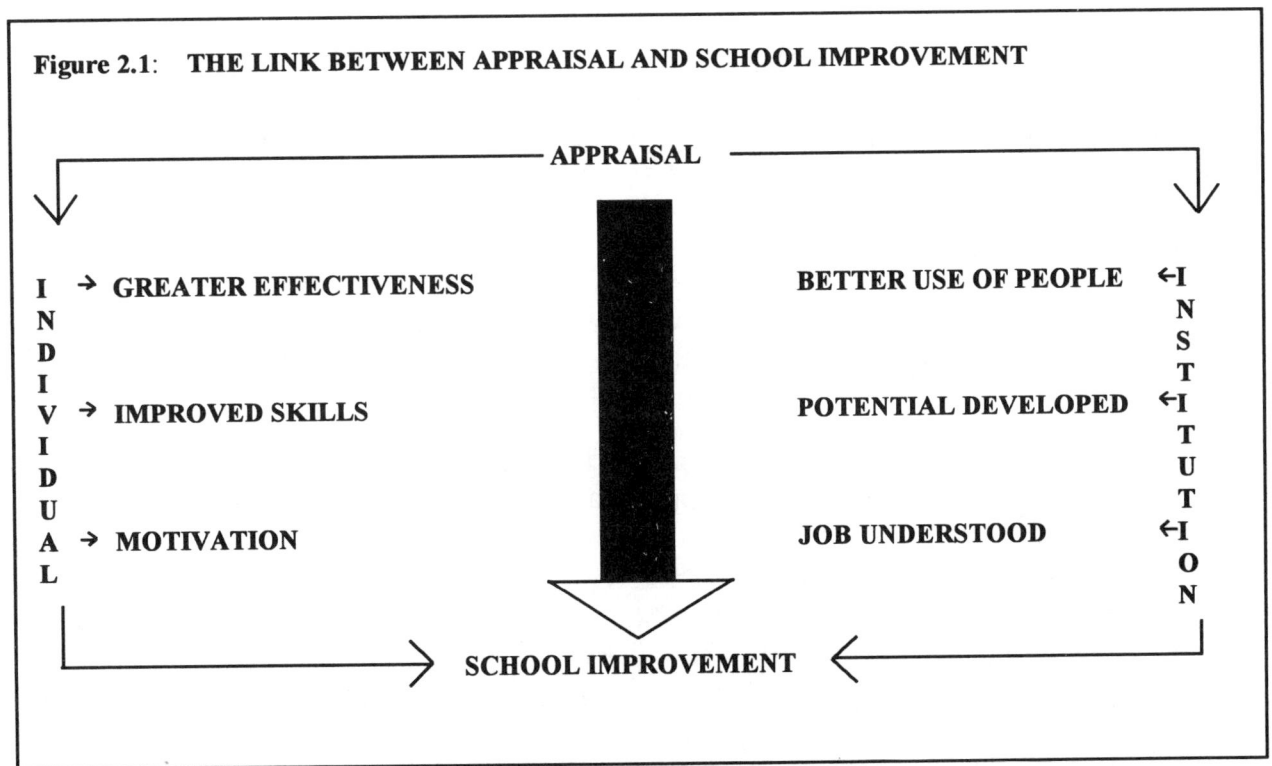

Figure 2.1: THE LINK BETWEEN APPRAISAL AND SCHOOL IMPROVEMENT

CHAPTER THREE

Planning for appraisal

In many schools there already exists a defined and coordinated policy for staff development which supports both individual and school needs. The aims of staff development closely match those of staff appraisal and a whole series of complementary processes and procedures is likely to be in evidence. For example, staff will be asked to complete self-review proformas in order to help identify needs; professional development coordinators may interview staff individually to discuss training needs in the context of the schools overall plan; INSET targets will be set.

The introduction of appraisal encourages schools to make such processes more coherent and systematic. Schools, in their implementation of appraisal should, wherever possible, build on the good practice which already exists and be less inclined to be dismissive of present routines. This will do much to establish a climate within which further development can take place. The pilot projects and subsequent practice in schools has provided significant evidence that the creation of a positive climate for the introduction of appraisal can best be accomplished through a whole-school approach. Within the Statutory Regulations schools can still enjoy the flexibility to make arrangements which reflect the schools ethos and particular philosophy of professional development.

It is of crucial importance that any appraisal scheme is carefully planned to fit in with the many initiatives currently taking place in schools. Planning and preparation for appraisal has to be thorough if the appraisee is to gain maximum benefit from the process and the appraiser is to help the appraisee achieve that benefit. Careful planning and preparation should enable both the appraisee and appraiser to come to the process in a confident, informed and positive frame of mind.

This chapter addresses the issues associated with the planning for and management of appraisal. It is based upon the assumptions that

- sound management strategies are essential to the successful development of appraisal;
- a well-managed appraisal programme can provide a firm grounding for other developments within the school.

Figure 3.1 below summarises for the reader the structure of the remainder of this chapter, as well as the three main steps of the planning process. Within each planning stage there are activities which you are invited to work through at your own pace. You may not, of course, find it necessary to work through each. The activities are appropriate for individuals who may be charged with establishing the school's arrangements for appraisal, e.g. the head teacher, deputy, appraisal/ staff development coordinator, and for small groups of staff, e.g. departments/faculties/areas/teams.

Figure 3.1: PLANNING FOR APPRAISAL

STEP 1: DEVELOPING A CONCEPT OF APPRAISAL	ACTIVITY 1: Developing a concept of appraisal	EXAMPLE 1
		EXAMPLE 2
STEP 2: DEVELOPING A FRAMEWORK FOR APPRAISAL	ACTIVITY 2: Generating ground-rules for appraisal	EXAMPLE 3
	ACTIVITY 3: Resolving organisational issues	EXAMPLE 4
	ACTIVITY 4: Responding to the questions of colleagues	EXAMPLE 5
STEP 3: IMPLEMENTING THE APPRAISAL ARRANGEMENTS	ACTIVITY 5: Creating a climate for appraisal	EXAMPLE 6
	ACTIVITY 6: Selecting the appraisers	EXAMPLE 7
	ACTIVITY 7: Developing a timetable	EXAMPLE 8
	ACTIVITY 8: Formulating job descriptions	EXAMPLE 9
	ACTIVITY 9: Training for appraisers and appraisees	EXAMPLE 10
	ACTIVITY 10: Supporting the appraisal process	EXAMPLE 11
		EXAMPLE 12
		EXAMPLE 13

STEP 1: DEVELOPING A CONCEPT OF APPRAISAL

For appraisal to stand any chance of being successful in schools, it will have to be perceived by teachers as an initiative which leads not only to higher standards of education for pupils, but also to their own professional development and individual fulfilment. Securing the commitment of all staff is a crucial first step in the school's planning strategy for appraisal.

Developing the school's own concept of appraisal is a vital pre-requisite to the scheme's growth and development. The following activity **(ACTIVITY 1)** attempts to raise the issues which may form the basis for your school's decision-making processes on implementing an appraisal strategy, and in turn to help you articulate your own particular philosophy of appraisal.

ACTIVITY 1: DEVELOPING A CONCEPT OF APPRAISAL

What does your school mean by appraisal?
How does this fit in with your overall staff development plan and your evaluation strategy?
Describe your concept of appraisal.

A system of appraisal must be supportive and constructive for the school and for each individual member of staff. The scheme decided upon should be based on the fundamentals of staff development. It is important to articulate such a concept of appraisal at the outset. The following are examples of the publicly stated concepts of appraisal in two schools:

EXAMPLE 1: A HIGH SCHOOL'S CONCEPT OF APPRAISAL

The School sees appraisal as a right of all teachers, something which is done with people rather than to them. It is therefore important that both appraisees and appraisers are actively involved in the process. Rather than adding to the already considerable pressures faced by staff, appraisal of performance should channel the energies of staff towards the essential rather than the superficial.

The principal aim of appraisal is to enhance and maximise the educational opportunities of pupils through the professional development of teachers, thus leading to both institutional and individual growth.

EXAMPLE 2: A MIDDLE SCHOOL'S CONCEPT OF APPRAISAL

Appraisal will enable staff to perform with greater self-knowledge and competence over the full range of their professional responsibilities in order to offer quality educational experience to students. It will provide a further opportunity for two-way communication between all levels in the school. It will lead to greater mutual awareness of the concerns and expectations of both appraiser and appraisee. The process will provide a Headteacher with a clearer, more detailed overview of staff performance which will assist him in planning curriculum and staff development.

STEP 2: DEVELOPING A FRAMEWORK FOR APPRAISAL

To facilitate the process of establishing a formative system of appraisal, acceptable guidelines must be laid down early on. A good school climate is vitally important for the implementation of teacher appraisal. The quality of management and accompanying processes need to be of the very highest order if the school is to deal successfully with the very sensitive and far-reaching organisational issues. The following section encourages you to address key issues in developing a framework for appraisal.

■   Generating ground rules

ACTIVITY 2: GENERATING GROUND RULES FOR APPRAISAL

Generate a set of ground rules for your appraisal programme. You should try to think of the underlying principles which would need to be clarified at the start of the process.

Although any system of appraisal must be retained within the bounds of professional development, certain ethical parameters must be clearly established before a scheme is introduced. Consideration needs to be given to areas such as confidentiality, the right to appeal, the scope of the information requested, access to records and information.

The feedback which results from the appraisal process should be to the mutual benefit of both appraiser and appraisee. Appraisal allows teachers to know how well they are doing, offering a fair and objective means of evaluating their performance. The same process informs the appraiser how well he or she is supporting the development of the teacher. In this context, both parties will be in a better position to prepare plans for development and improvement in an atmosphere which is formative, supportive and developmental.

An effective overall appraisal of the teacher needs to be developed by appraising the teacher in a range of contexts, covering a whole cross-section of situations which comprise the essence of the teacher's job, thus providing a comprehensive profile of the teachers performance. However, such a profile can only reasonably be formed over an extended period of time. Regular appraisal of the performance of teachers facilitates the on-going review of the effectiveness and efficiency with which resources are utilized. Such a review is not restricted to those commonly identified resources such as finance and equipment but to resource-related issues such as teacher time, training and administration.

Appraisal, by its very nature, will highlight matters which do not lend themselves easily to precise measurement. Schools will need to consider complementary approaches for quantifying what may be reasonably quantified. However, to be credible, the process should be based on objective criteria wherever possible.

To succeed in practice, appraisal must be perceived not only as a means of enhancing the quality of teaching and learning but also as an opportunity for the professional development and individual fulfilment of every teacher. One important way of encouraging teachers to accept appraisal as a non-threatening activity is for them to feel involved in the process and decision-making. Each stage in the process - preparation, observation, interviewing and subsequent follow-up - needs to be an area of active participation and negotiation by both appraisers and appraisees. Appraisal can only become effective when mutually agreed objectives are negotiated within the institutional context.

Whilst appraisal is a key feature in the process of identifying professional needs, it represents a key development activity in itself. The establishment of an appraisal system requires appropriate training and development relevant to the process itself. All participants will, therefore, require training in skills and methods appropriate to their background, role, and experience.

In order to establish and maintain a positive attitude towards appraisal, it is crucial that all teachers are fully informed about both policy and procedures. The aims of the scheme must be made clear to all involved, and steps taken to ensure that this understanding is shared by all the staff. This needs to begin as early as possible in the decision-making stages.

To satisfy managerial, developmental and accountability demands schemes of appraisal will need to harmonise both the procedures and the outcomes of the process. This perspective views teacher appraisal as a vital precondition for successful professional development.

The following examples are of ground rules generated by three schools:

EXAMPLE 3: GROUND RULES ESTABLISHED BY A HIGH SCHOOL

Ground Rules

1. *All full-time staff will be appraised for a whole year. Part-time staff employed for a whole year for 0.4 of the week will be appraised.*
2. *The procedure must be formulated after consultation. The appraisee must be actively involved in the process, each stage of which needs to be an area of active participation and negotiation between those involved.*
3. *The procedure, including areas for appraisal, criteria, outcomes and reports must be clear at the outset.*
4. *Appraisal should benefit both appraiser and appraisee.*
5. *Appraisal should be over the full range of the appraisee's duties and responsibilities as defined in the appraisee's job description.*
6. *The appraisee should have the opportunity, if he or she wishes, at the initial meeting and/or at the appraisal interview, of initiating discussion of his/her non-contractual (voluntary) contribution and also her/his career aspirations.*
7. *The process will be hierarchical - i.e. the appraiser will be of higher status or allowance than the appraisee.*
8. *Wherever possible, the appraisee should be able to choose whether he/she is appraised by someone of the same subject discipline or by someone of a different subject discipline. Most Heads of Faculty and some Heads of Department will not have this choice, since there will be no one senior to them with the same subject discipline.*
9. *All meetings between appraiser and appraisee will take place at mutually agreed times and in the most appropriate room.*
10. *Although the appraiser retains the right to observe any lesson, the decision as to which groups/lessons are to be observed will be the result of discussion/negotiation at the initial meeting.*
11. *The appraisal process has as high a priority as is reasonably possible - i.e. decisions as to which lessons are observed are not unduly influenced by the appraiser's timetable and whether or not supply cover will be required.*
12. *The appraisers must receive appropriate training in the skills required - e.g. listening, interviewing, negotiation, target setting, action planning, etc.*
13. *Rules of confidentiality:*
    a. All discussions at any meeting/interview between the appraiser and appraisee must remain confidential to the two people involved.
    b. The final agreed statement must remain confidential to the appraiser, the appraisee and to the Headteacher. It may (with the consent of the appraisee) be shown to the appraisee's Head of Faculty and/or Head of Department
    c. Care must be taken to ensure confidentiality in the preparation and storage of the appraisal system.
    d. The Chair of Governors has access, on request, to the targets for the whole staff but not to the appraisal report of a particular member of staff.
14. *Right of Appeal*
    The Complaints Procedure has now been agreed between the LEA and the Professional Associations, and has been made available to staff.
15. *After considering analyses of specimen self-appraisal statements conducted by staff, the headteacher and appraisal coordinator have agreed on an appropriate format, a copy of which is attached*

EXAMPLE 4: GROUND RULES ESTABLISHED BY A MIDDLE SCHOOL

1.   *Confidentiality of what is discussed or noted is essential.*
2.   *The focus should be on a key school area rather than an individual member of staff.*
3.   *More than one appraiser permitted for each member of staff.*
4.   *Objections to appraiser permitted (negative choices of appraiser[s]) if staff so wish.*
5.   *Positive support mechanism*
6.   *Whole process is negotiable between appraisers and appraisee.*

EXAMPLE 5: GROUND RULES ESTABLISHED BY A SPECIAL SCHOOL

1.   *The teacher's job description must clearly state the responsibilities of the post, and should hopefully be acceptable to both the head and the teacher.*
2.   *The appraiser should be a person acceptable to the appraisee.*
3.   *The appraiser should be trained for the task and thus generate trust and credibility.*
4.   *The appraisal policy, procedures and aims, should be made clear at the outset.*
5.   *Appraisal should be regarded as purposeful and formative and lead to appropriate in-service training.*
6.   *The outcome of the appraisal should be that the appraisee knows how well he/she is performing in the school situation and has positive plans for training and development both in the present situation and in the future. Likewise the appraiser should recognise the contribution which he/she has made and can continue to give the appraisee.*

■   **Organisational issues**

The organisational structure for appraisal will have to differ widely between schools. There is no one correct structure; each school will need to tailor its system to suit its own context, ethos, and stage of development.

Below is an activity which you may find useful when considering the organisational issues associated with appraisal:

ACTIVITY 3: RESOLVING ORGANISATIONAL ISSUES WITHIN THE SCHOOL

What organisational issues does appraisal present you with?
How do you propose to build trust and establish understanding about the system?

Here are some examples of possible organisational arrangements which schools may choose to use:

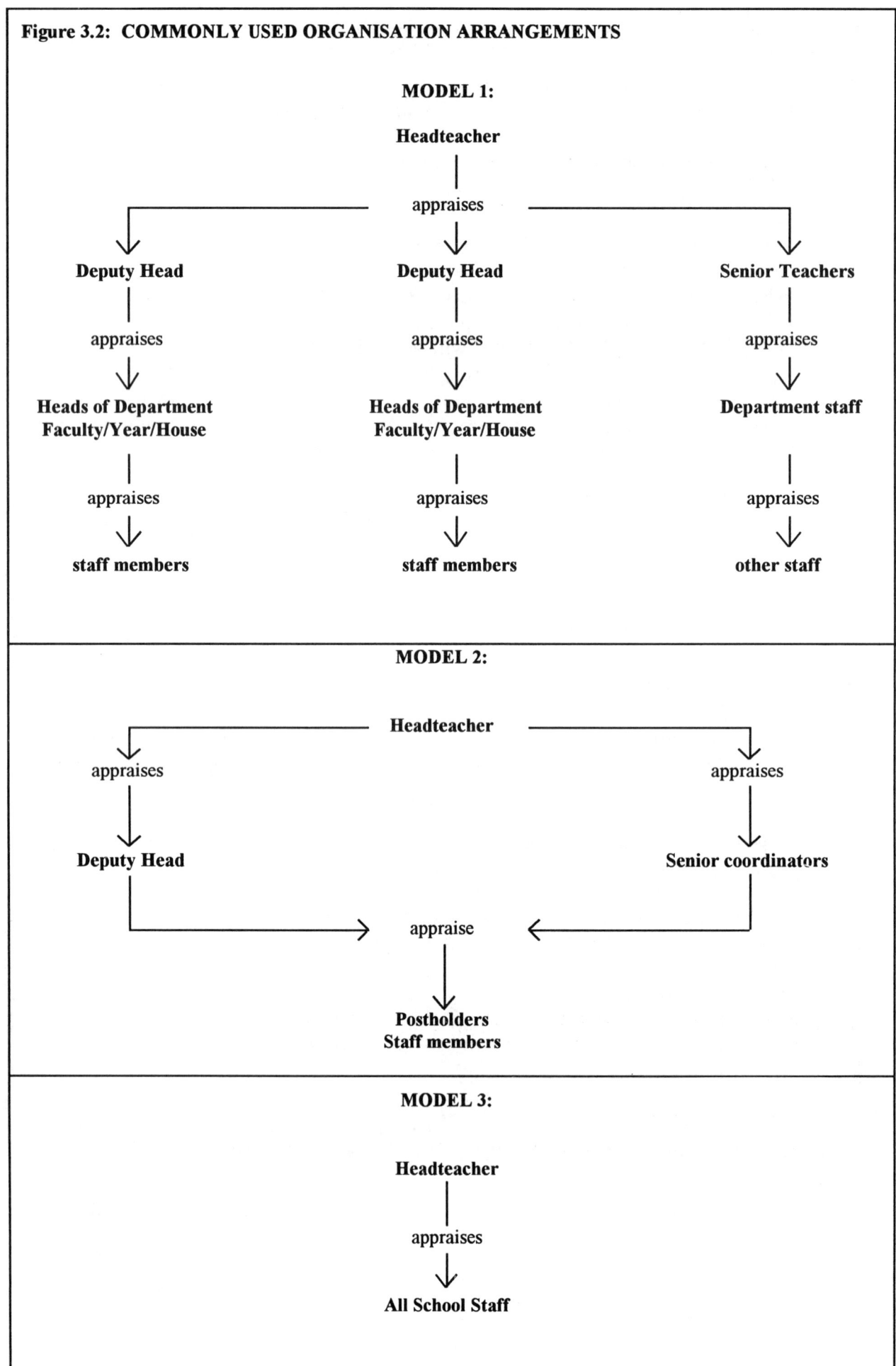

Figure 3.2: COMMONLY USED ORGANISATION ARRANGEMENTS

MODEL 1:

Headteacher

appraises

Deputy Head

Deputy Head

Senior Teachers

appraises

appraises

appraises

Heads of Department
Faculty/Year/House

Heads of Department
Faculty/Year/House

Department staff

appraises

appraises

appraises

staff members

staff members

other staff

MODEL 2:

Headteacher

appraises

appraises

Deputy Head

Senior coordinators

appraise

Postholders
Staff members

MODEL 3:

Headteacher

appraises

All School Staff

■ Implications for managers of the appraisal process

The implementation of appraisal arrangements poses many important questions for managers. The following questions may serve as a useful checklist for managers:

- What are the benefits of appraisal?
- How will the school carry out a whole-school review?
- Have job descriptions been provided for all staff?
- Which members of staff will be appraisers?
- How will appraisers be matched with appraisees?
- What skills will need to be developed by appraisees and appraisers?
- How will the components of the appraisal cycle be managed?
- What support materials/guidelines will be made available?
- How will the needs which arise from the appraisal process be met?

Responding with confidence, accuracy and tact to the queries of colleagues is another vital role for managers of the appraisal arrangements in schools.

ACTIVITY 4: RESPONDING TO THE QUESTIONS OF COLLEAGUES

Generate a list of questions to which staff in your school are likely to require answers. How will you respond to each?

An effective appraisal programme requires a great deal of organisation, as well as sensitivity in the way in which it is managed. Putting the appraisal scheme into action is the responsibility of senior management, and as such must be perceived as an integral part of future management practice. The following issues need to be resolved before an appraisal programme can be put into action:

- Who will conduct the appraisal?
- What training will there be for appraiser and appraisee?
- What will be appraised and what criteria will be used?
- What data will be collected for the appraisal?
- What use will be made of the appraisal record?
- What time will be available for the process?
- How will appraisal influence the management and organisation of the school?
- How will appraisal influence decisions on promotion?

■ Establishing a climate for appraisal

The point about the climate is important. I think you need to judge when a school is ready for appraisal. The word appraisal will have some faintly sinister connotations in the minds of some teachers, threatening assessment on a five-point scale or reminding them of their teaching practice days when someone sat at the back of the lesson to "criticize", or, worse still, assisting the process of weeding out the much talked about incompetent section of the profession.

Nicholson, 1984

Because appraisal comes so much closer to a teacher's performance, personal qualities and beliefs than possibly any other initiative, it is seen as an extremely delicate issue. The importance of climate in the introduction of appraisal must therefore never be underestimated. It is important at the outset to gauge the existing climate of opinion and feeling because this will affect the nature of the awareness-raising which follows. A favourable climate is likely to be one in which there is trust and openness between those involved, a recognition that there are different perspectives dependent, amongst other things, upon the contexts in which people work - and a good communications system. If the degree of mutual trust and understanding is less than perfect, then awareness-raising has to begin by creating it.

Letting people know what is going to happen simply isn't enough in appraisal. It has to be set in context, clarifying its purpose and signifying the likely outcomes. It must be made clear that appraisal is a two-way process, a partnership, concerned not only with the teacher's work in the classroom and in the school, but also with the role of management in facilitating that work, through appropriate organisation, adequate resourcing, the provision of support and opportunities for professional development. A discussion of these issues rapidly makes one aware that appraisal may begin with teachers but its effects extend to pupils and the schools in which they work.

ACTIVITY 5 below invites you to consider the delicate, yet crucial, issue of climate and to consider to what extent there are existing practices which may offer a platform on which to build your appraisal arrangements:

ACTIVITY 5: CREATING A CLIMATE FOR APPRAISAL

Appraisal needs to be conducted in an atmosphere of trust and openness if it is to enjoy the support of staff.
What are the characteristics of the existing climate? Which of these in particular would you wish to build upon?

■   **Selecting the appraisers of teachers**

An important decision for the head of the school will be the matching of appraisers with appraisees. In carrying out **ACTIVITY 6** below, you will need to take account of the alternatives available to you:

•   the headteacher acts as appraiser for all staff

•   the headteacher does not act as an appraiser but sees all staff for a discussion of professional development targets

•   a hierarchical structure is adopted with Deputies, Heads of Departments/Year/House/Section, Coordinators, Teachers with special responsibility for subjects appraising staff for whom they are responsible

- appraisal is developed through departmental/faculty/team/area peer groups

- a "bottom-up" approach is adopted

- in schools with fewer than four or five teachers a clustering arrangement between several schools may be helpful, especially where an outside view might be sought.

ACTIVITY 6: SELECTING THE APPRAISERS

How do you intend to approach this issue?
Make a list of possible appraisers for your school.
Who would appraise whom?
What factors do you need to take into account in coming to these decisions?

In introducing appraisal, schools should build on existing good practice. In some schools this may be seen as department-based and so peer-group appraisal may seem an obvious structure to explore. At the end of the first cycle, the staff will need to consider the perceived disadvantages of the process, particularly that of credibility, in order to answer possible critics. This evaluation may result in an appraisal process which is a mixture of peer-group/hierarchical or which is peer-group with moderation from someone outside the department or school. Although all schools will share general principles, the system which is introduced should derive from the context of the school and the policies for staff development which already exist.

In schools where there is a collaborative approach to school management, the notion of a hierarchical system of appraisal may well seem to be at odds with the school culture. Peer-group appraisal might be a workable alternative in situations such as:

- deputy headteachers acting as appraisers for colleague deputies in the same or indeed other schools;
- heads of departments/coordinators acting as appraisers for colleague heads of departments/coordinators;
- members of departments appraising each other in the context of agreed departmental policies;
- members of departments appraising their head of department.

Such a system has the advantage of:

- supporting existing staff development structures within the school
- taking some of the threat, as perceived by some staff, out of appraisal
- being relatively easy to arrange and monitor
- matching individual, department and school targets

The disadvantages are:

- that peer-group appraisal may serve to reinforce practice which is not good

- that peer-group appraisal may be cosy and not challenging
- that departmental perspectives may overshadow the needs and expectations of the individual and the school
- that peer-group appraisal can lack credibility with parents and governors.

Figure 3.3: LINE-MANAGEMENT AND PEER APPRAISAL APPROACHES COMPARED

Line-management appraisal	Peer appraisal
• ensures appraiser is better informed about the teacher at interview • keeps the process streamlined • may be seen as threatening • line-manager may not necessarily be a good teacher • line-manager may not have experience of teaching all the areas taught by the teacher	• appraiser could be someone with a proven expertise in an area of interest to the teacher • can be less threatening than observation by line manager • can result in appraiser not having as good a picture of the teacher when the interview takes place • peer may not be in a position to facilitate any actions suggested by the appraisal

---

EXAMPLE 6: A HIGH SCHOOL'S POLICY ON THE SELECTION OF APPRAISERS

The Headteacher will appraise the Deputy Heads and "E" post holders. The Senior Management Team (Headteacher and two Deputies plus 2 "E" postholders) will appraise the five "D" postholders. The "D" postholders will be able to indicate the names of any two members of the SMT whom they would prefer as appraisers. All other staff will be able to indicate whether they wish to be appraised by their direct line-manager (i.e. Head of Faculty or Head of Department) or by a member of the Senior Management Team. If they choose the latter option they (like the "D" postholders) will be able to indicate the names of any two members of the SMT they would prefer. The Headteacher and Appraisal Co-ordinator will then draw up the list of appraisers. This will include all members of the SMT, and all "D" postholders (Heads of Faculty). It is also likely to include some Heads of Department.

EXAMPLE 7: A JUNIOR SCHOOL'S APPROACH TO THE SELECTION OF APPRAISERS

Memo to all staff

APPRAISAL

You will remember our introduction to appraisal given at the Training Day in September and my reference to the subject at the Staff Meeting in October. After much careful deliberation with members of staff I have decided that the first two years of the cycle will be as "user friendly" as it is possible to make it. Hence I am proposing that your appraiser will be:

In addition, I would like you to be the appraiser for:

This information is given to you for the moment in strictest confidence. If you have any observations to make I would be grateful if you would let me have them no later than... It is my intention that the full list will be published in the Staff Bulletin on...

Thereafter, it will, of course, be quite proper for appraisee and appraiser to make informal contact and agree on their future timetable.

■ **Timetable**

Finding and allocating time to accommodate the profusion of initiatives currently facing schools is difficult, to say the very least. Yet, many schools are taking this opportunity of evaluating their existing routines and practices in an attempt to rationalise. In some schools time has already been allocated to the reviewing and planning process for the School Development Plan. This may provide a useful starting point for the introduction of appraisal. Ways in which this can be achieved include

- blocking the timetable
- using directed time
- using test/examination periods
- adding to the length of the school day
- using lunchtimes
- using work experience time
- using auxiliary help - financed from the school budget, e.g. for examination invigilation, swimming, etc
- using time twice - during departmental reviews or curriculum discussion times
- using Teacher Education Days
- reassessing the effectiveness and efficiency of the current meetings pattern and setting some of this time aside for aspects of the appraisal cycle, e.g. initial meeting.

ACTIVITY 7 invites you to consider the timetabling issue and - with the assistance of the schools calendar of events, a staff list, etc - to map out a timetable which would ensure that the required number of staff is being appraised in accordance with the DfE's guidelines. Some illustrations are set out in Examples 8, 9 and 10 below.

ACTIVITY 7: DEVELOPING A TIMETABLE

Develop a timetable for the first two years of the appraisal programme. Include in-service training provision within this timetable.

EXAMPLE 8: TIMETABLE FOR THE APPRAISAL PROCESS - HIGH SCHOOL

Consultation between working party members and faculty/departmental groups. Informal discussions with professional association representatives - by 12th June 1993

Revision/modification of all job descriptions by Headteacher and appraisal coordinator. Appraisers to be chosen and detailed schedule prepared for Autumn Term 1993 - by 17th July 1993

Initial meetings between appraiser and appraisee (for which self-appraisal proforma could provide a structure) - all completed by October half-term 1993

Classroom observation plus appraisal interview (including discussion of wider professional responsibilities and targets) - to be completed by Easter 1994

Appraisal statements and targets to be prepared, agreed and handed to Headteacher - by July 1994

Review targets of each individual within a year

EXAMPLE 9: TIMETABLE FOR THE APPRAISAL PROCESS - MIDDLE SCHOOL

1993

2nd September	*Introduction to Appraisal - County Inspector for Appraisal*
20th December	*Teacher Education Day*

1994

14th February	*Publication of individual appraiser/appraisee pairings*
20th February	*Publication of full appraisal grid*
25th February	*Headteacher presentation at staff meeting including brief to Working Party*
31st March	*Working Party present recommendations*
6-10 April	*Headteacher and Deputy meetings with appraisers*
13th April	*Headteacher meeting with all appraisers*
13-15 April	*Issue of job descriptions*
1st June	*Dissemination and completion of self-review proforma*
1-12 June	*Initial meeting for appraisers and appraisees*
15th June - *30th Sept*	*Classroom observation and collection of relevant information*
30th Sept - *5th Oct*	*Training sessions - appraisal interviewing*
w/c 6th Nov	*Preparation of appraisal statements and targets*

1995

July	*Follow-up and formal review meetings*

EXAMPLE 10: TIMETABLE FOR THE APPRAISAL PROCESS - FIRST SCHOOL

<u>*YEAR ONE*</u>   *Appraiser   -   Headteacher*
                Appraisees   -   4 staff including Deputy Head

SEPTEMBER 1992   *Self appraisal sheet given to appraisees*

OCTOBER 1992   *Initial meetings*
                Classroom observations

NOVEMBER 1992   *Appraisal meeting*
                Report and target setting

<u>*YEAR TWO*</u>   *Appraiser   -   Deputy Head*
                Appraisees   -   3 staff

SEPTEMBER 1993   *Self appraisal sheet given to appraisees*

OCTOBER 1993   *Year review with appraisees*
                Initial meetings
                Classroom observations

NOVEMBER 1993   *Appraisal meeting*
                Report and target setting

<u>*YEAR THREE*</u>   *Appraiser   -   Deputy Head*
                Appraisees   -   4 staff plus Head to appraise Deputy Head

<u>*YEAR FOUR*</u>   *Appraiser   -   Headteacher*
                Appraisee   -   3 staff

◉ Job descriptions

It is important that all staff, including the headteacher, should have clear descriptions of what is expected of them, drawn up in consultation with interested parties. The value of any job description as a practical document will depend largely on who was involved in its development and how it was constructed. Other factors include the time and other resources available, the experience of the holder and the precise responsibilities agreed. For these and other reasons it must be remembered that all job descriptions have limitations. A job description, while providing a framework for action, does not provide guidance on how the role might be performed. A fuller consideration of job descriptions appears on page 35.

ACTIVITY 8: FORMULATING JOB DESCRIPTIONS

Central to any scheme of appraisal is the preparation of job descriptions. Do all staff have accurate and up to date job descriptions? If not, what is to be your strategy for dealing with this issue?

■ Training for appraisers and appraisees

It was made clear in the ACAS document that "all teachers should be trained to play their part in appraisal". The Government has made funding available via the Grants for Education Support & Training (GEST) initiative to support INSET in the area of appraisal.

Whereas teachers possess many of the requisite skills and currently engage in many of the processes, the successful introduction of a formal scheme of appraisal needs specific and focused INSET. There is considerable agreement that both appraisees and appraisers need training for appraisal. If a successful appraisal process relies upon the quality of the relationship between appraisee and appraiser, it is essential for both parties to be skilled in relationship building, and therefore the same type and amount of training is necessary.
A training strategy for appraisal involves:

- awareness-raising   -   general
                                        -     specific
- information giving
- skills training

In deciding the level and extent of training required it will be crucial to consider the following questions:

- Where is the school now in relation to appraisal?
- Where does the school need to be and by when?
- How well informed are the staff about appraisal?
- How much time and money does the school have to invest in the training associated with the initiative?
- What outcomes and benefits are expected as a result of the training?
- Is the outlay of time and money congruent with the expected benefits and outcomes?
- Is there an acceptance by the staff that new knowledge, skills and understanding are required in order to implement the appraisal scheme?
- Have the barriers to change and the anxiety of staff been taken into account in planning the training strategy?
- How does the training associated with appraisal fit with the overall INSET programme planned for the institution?

Training for appraisees should aim to:

- explain the framework set out in the Regulation and Circular, the LEA's own scheme, the role of the appraiser and appraisee, and the relationship between appraisal and the development plan for the school
- introduce teachers to the skills they will need to participate effectively
- cover all practical aspects of appraisal

Training for appraisers should aim to:

- explain in detail the principles and practice of the LEA scheme
- emphasise that appraisal should be seen as an integral element in the management of

the school
- help to develop appropriate skills
- cover all practical aspects of appraisal

Experience during the pilot projects suggests a need for sustained on-the-job assistance. Whereas training courses can provide basic understanding, training is likely to be more meaningful when taking place back in school, with practical experience and feedback. It is important to cater for this need when allocating resources. The use of video has proved to be a powerful training medium, providing stimulus for trainees and enabling recording of performance and provision of feedback during training. Training can influence proposals for a school appraisal scheme and therefore help to provide a sense of ownership. Important ingredients of effective training seem to be: the variety of methods used, e.g. describing, modelling, practising and coaching new skills; active learning; flexibility; non-threatening activities; credible trainers; comfortable surroundings; and a short time span between training and practice.

ACTIVITY 9: TRAINING FOR APPRAISERS AND APPRAISEES

Who will need training and at what level?
What in-service training is likely to be needed by appraisers and appraisees?

EXAMPLE 11: A 2-DAY TRAINING PROGRAMME FOR THE SENIOR MANAGEMENT TEAM (10) OF A HIGH SCHOOL

TEACHER APPRAISAL - THEORY INTO PRACTICE

This two-day programme is designed to:

- *provide an update of the DES appraisal requirements*
- *help us become clearer about the purposes of appraisal*
- *help us consider appropriate structures*
- *provide us with opportunities to practise the skills needed*
- *help us consider the links between appraisal and the school plan*
- *help us clarify criteria against which appraisal might take place*

EXAMPLE 12: A WHOLE-SCHOOL AWARENESS-RAISING PROGRAMME

9.00   *Introduction*
         DES Regulations
         LEA Guidelines

10.00   *Group Task*
         What do you think will be the outcomes of the appraisal process for pupils, for you, for the school?
         What are your concerns about appraisal as appraisee, as appraiser?

10.50   *Coffee*

11.15   *Plenary - comments on flip charts*

11.30   *The Appraisal Cycle*
         Individual/group task
         What are your criteria for selection of your own appraiser?

12.15   *Plenary*

12.30   *Lunch*

1.30   *Components of the Appraisal Cycle*
         Initial meeting/collection of information/self appraisal
         Appraisal interviews
         Negotiating statements and targets
         Follow-up

3.30   *Plenary*

4.00   *Close*

■   Ongoing support

Participants in the appraisal process are likely to be engaged in a personal learning experience and will require ongoing support in order to gain maximum benefit from the process. Such support may come from the school's coordinator for appraisal (usually a member of the senior management team) as he/she attempts to help staff reflect upon the experience that colleagues have of the process, to distil from it the most significant lessons and to spread examples of good practice. A second level of support relates to the staff development arising from the outcomes of appraisal rather than the process itself.

ACTIVITY 10: SUPPORTING THE APPRAISAL PROCESS

What support will be required to introduce the appraisal programme successfully?

The following is an appraisal policy document which was developed partly as a result of following the activities contained in this chapter:

EXAMPLE 13: AN EXTRACT FROM A SCHOOL APPRAISAL POLICY

1. WHY WE SHOULD UNDERTAKE STAFF APPRAISAL

The School is committed to maintaining and, wherever possible, improving the quality of every aspect of its work. You, the staff, are the Schools most important asset and the appraisal scheme is intended to be an investment in you. The scheme is designed to benefit all staff, individually, by helping you systematically to review your performance and identify ways of further improving performance and job satisfaction. It is also intended to benefit you collectively through the improvement in the quality of the Schools performance which will result from individual appraisal. Our scheme has the following specific objectives:

- *to enhance the current performance of individuals and the quality of teaching and learning;*
- *to raise the level of job satisfaction;*
- *to agree individual performance targets and action plans;*
- *to review past performance with a view to identifying personal and organisational factors which have influenced performance;*
- *to encourage activities which contribute to professional and personal development within the context of the School;*
- *to provide an opportunity for structured feedback and discussion.*

2. HOW THE SCHEME WILL WORK

Of vital importance to the success of the scheme is the manner in which the scheme is planned and organised. The following principles should be self-evident to all staff within the School, but are so important that they are set out below:

- *Openness - appraisal will be conducted in a frank and honest way which encourages constructive dialogue between appraiser and appraisee based on as wide a range of evidence about performance as possible.*
- *Confidentiality - scrupulous care will be taken to ensure confidentiality. Appraisers will not discuss the contents of the appraisal itself with anyone other than the appropriate appraisee without their prior agreement. Special care will be taken to maintain the confidential aspects of all written evidence and records.*
- *Equal Opportunity - all aspects of the appraisal process will be conducted without discriminating on grounds of gender, race, or marital status. In addition, every care will be taken to avoid stereo-typed expectations.*
- *Consistency of values and standards - all staff within the School are important and appraisal will be conducted with equal care and seriousness for every colleague whatever their role or status.*
- *Self-appraisal - all staff are encouraged to undertake a continuous process of professional self-reflection. Drawing upon this as the start of appraisal will form the cornerstone of the process.*
- *Implementing the outcomes - to be of maximum benefit all those involved must ensure that they do their utmost to implement the plans which are produced as a result of the appraisal process. The onus for this will vary according to circumstances but both appraiser and appraisee should recognise their responsibilities here.*
- *Training - appraisal is an important activity and all staff, appraisers and appraisees, will undertake appraisal training before involvement in the process to help ensure they operate the system to maximum benefit.*
- *Review - the essence of appraisal is review, with a view to identifying opportunities for improving performance. This will also apply to the appraisal process which will be reviewed regularly drawing on feedback from all involved.*

The programme of ten activities contained in this chapter will have ensured that the reader has taken account of the major issues which affect the implementation of appraisal. Together they will have provided a structure for the development of an appraisal policy for the organisation.

CHAPTER FOUR

The Appraisal Cycle: Teachers

In broad terms, appraisal comprises gathering information about the professional performance of the teacher, jointly reviewing this information, and then planning future action and support to aid his or her development. The School Teacher Appraisal Regulations and Circular 12/91 have presented a model of appraisal which is cyclical and therefore continuous. Essentially, it comprises three main phases: preparation, interview and follow-up. There may be occasions when the continuity of the two-year cycle may be interrupted or broken.

The following paragraphs from the DfE Circular 12/91 clarify the situation with regard to teachers who are internally promoted, leave to join the staff of another school, or who are given acting responsibilities within their current school.

CIRCULAR 12/91: THE APPRAISAL CYCLE

para.

12.   The Regulations provide for appraisal to take place on a two year cycle.

13.   The appraisal cycle should start afresh if a school teacher moves to a post in a different school. If a school teacher moves to a new post within the same school, there is discretion as to whether to start the appraisal cycle again or carry on the existing cycle. Much will depend on how similar the responsibilities of the new post are to those of the old post, the stage during the appraisal cycle at which the move takes place, and whether the appraiser would have to change.

14.   If a school teacher is
- substantively promoted to head teacher in the middle of the appraisal cycle, whether in the same school or not, the appraisal cycle should begin again;
- given acting promotion to head teacher in the middle of the appraisal cycle, the Regulations leave the appraising body with discretion as to whether to start the appraisal cycle again, or to continue with the current cycle.

Implementation Timetable

Responsibility for the implementation of appraisal has been given to the appraising bodies - LEAs or governing bodies. They are planning to ensure that at least half of their teachers will have had their observation and appraisal interview during the school years 1992/93 and 1994/95. Teachers appointed after 1st September 1991 have been given a further year's grace, as have governors of grant-maintained schools.

CIRCULAR 12/91: TIMETABLE
para.
15.   The timetable ... is intended to secure an orderly phase-in, whilst leaving appraising bodies
        with some flexibility.   The two key targets for the appraising body in Regulation 6 mean that
        i.   a number of school teachers equal to half the number of school teachers for whom they
        were responsible on 1st September 1991 must complete the first year of the appraisal cycle at
        some time during the school year 1992/93 (i.e. - they must have had their observation and
        appraisal interview); and
        ii.   all school teachers for whom they were responsible on 1st September 1991 must complete
        the first year of the appraisal cycle during the school year 1994/95.
16.   If a school becomes grant-maintained during the phase-in period, the Regulations require all
        school teachers who have started the appraisal cycle to continue with it without a break.
        Because of the change of appraising body, other school teachers in such schools will not be
        caught by the deadlines in Regulations 6(1) and 6(2).   By virtue of Regulation 6(4), all such
        school teachers will have to be the subject of appraisal from 1st September 1995.   Schools
        which become grant-maintained may introduce their school teachers in advance of this
        deadline if they wish.

For schools and colleges which are building their appraisal strategy on a platform of a sound climate, clear goals, appropriate management, and effective staff development, the time-line proposed by the Regulation is unlikely to prove as much of a problem as it might for institutions where these pre-requisites are less well developed. In some cases the LEA will have decided on a phased implementation of appraisal within its schools and colleges. For example, in Hereford & Worcester appraisal has been introduced as follows:

Figure 4.1: AN LEA'S PLAN FOR THE PHASED IMPLEMENTATION OF APPRAISAL

YEAR PHASE	1991-92	1992-93	1993-94	1994-95
HIGH	✓			
MIDDLE/ PRIMARY/ SPECIAL		✓		
PRIMARY			✓	

The reason for this phase division was that approximately half the teaching population was located in the secondary sector. Secondary school colleagues had, by chance, received more training and had carried out more preparation for appraisal. Furthermore, since the focus of many of the latest innovations had been on primary schools, it allowed the LEA an opportunity to offer them a period of consolidation before introducing yet another initiative.

34

Equal Opportunities

```
CIRCULAR 12/91: EQUAL OPPORTUNITIES
para.
17.     Appraisal must operate, and be seen to operate, fairly and equitably for all school teachers.
        Appraisers should bear in mind their responsibility under the law not to discriminate on
        grounds of sex, race or marital status in the way in which they conduct appraisal; and the
        dangers of stereotyped expectations which result in a biassed approach.
18.     Training for appraisal, appraisal itself and professional development generally should be used
        positively to promote equal opportunities by encouraging all school teachers to fulfil their
        potential.  Appraisers should, for example, actively encourage all school teachers, including
        women teachers and teachers from the ethnic minorities, who have management potential to
        consider applying for management posts.
```

The National Steering Group properly placed fair and equitable treatment for all teachers at the centre of the process and stated outright that appraisal should be used positively to promote equal opportunities by encouraging all teachers to fulfil their potential. The Circular draws attention to the dangers of stereotyped expectations. Training should emphasise that appraisal offers an opportunity to encourage all teachers with appropriate potential to apply for senior posts.

A commitment such as this is often reflected in a school's or LEA's Equal Opportunities Policy. For example, the following statement is taken from an LEA policy:

"Equal opportunities is central to, and inseparable from that high quality education which is appropriate in the interests, needs and entitlements of the people of Warwickshire; it is the basis of good educational practice and good management, not simply an optional extra. Equal Opportunities is about rights, fairness and justice; it is about ensuring that the available pool of talent and ability is fully used and developed..."

(Warwickshire Equal Opportunities Policy, 1991)

Work to be Appraised

```
CIRCULAR 12/91: WORK TO BE APPRAISED
para.
19.     The appraiser is entitled to appraise performance across the full range of professional duties
        undertaken, including temporary responsibilities.  Appraisal should be undertaken on the
        basis of an established job description.
20.     Appraisal is likely to be more purposeful if it focuses on specific areas of a school teachers
        work.  This will be particularly so with the appraisal of head teachers, deputy heads and
        other teachers with a wide range of managerial duties.
```

To do justice to the wide diversity of a teacher's role is clearly difficult and, realistically, appraisal alone cannot cover all aspects of a teacher's contribution to the life and work of the school. A more realistic approach is to focus on one, two or three clearly identified, and agreed, aspects of the appraisee's work. Focusing on more than three aspects should be avoided.

Job Descriptions

In identifying the scope of any particular appraisal cycle it will be useful for both the appraisee and appraiser to reflect upon the appraisee's job description. This avoids the situation quoted below:

> You are probably being judged by certain criteria that would be news to you. And you are probably making certain contributions that would be news to them.
>
> Mark McCormack *(What They Didn't Teach You at the Harvard Business School,* 1989)

Basically, a job description describes an individual teacher's professional duties, responsibilities and status within the school. It also provides appropriate information to other colleagues within the school about whom and for whom the teacher is responsible. A good job description is one which is clear, concise and informative.

Increasingly, schools have come to view job descriptions as open documents so that all staff are aware of where the responsibility for areas of organisation and activity lies. This same openness, involving consultation with staff, will be required in preparing for the introduction of appraisal.

Job descriptions are crucial to the appraisal process; teacher and headteacher appraisal should be *"undertaken on the basis of an established job description"*. Such a document provides useful reference points for appraising performance, and is a basis for setting targets which will help individual staff development.

The basis of a job description is the teacher's contract of employment and the duties laid down in the relevant *School Teachers' Pay and Conditions* document. The description can then be used to clarify specific as well as general responsibilities.

As with appraisal, the development of job descriptions will be considerably eased if there is a spirit of cooperation and trust among the staff. The sense of ownership and confidence needed to facilitate the process should not be underestimated. The process of drawing up job descriptions, or reviewing existing ones, should balance the needs of the school with the preferences and aspirations of the individual. Consequently, whole school discussion, which identifies school development priorities, will encourage staff ownership of the development plan and help ensure that the development, or review, of the job descriptions contributes to the achievement of the identified aims.

Many schools, especially larger ones, have created generic job descriptions for those with managerial responsibilities, while allowing sufficient scope for adaptation according to individual circumstances. In short, the job description should include particulars like:

- job title and scale
- job conditions
- duties
- responsibilities

The core content of a job description is a definition of what the school expects from all staff to produce acceptable performance. This basic definition may be based on the following 5-point plan:

1. **Pastoral responsibilities**
2. **Teaching responsibilities**
3. **Personal skills development**
4. **Contribution to the department and school community**
5. **Administration**

Within each of these areas, it is possible to detail a number of specific accountabilities. Although school policies may describe each area in detail, it may be argued that they have a place in one document. A job description may also be used for self-review. A teacher is able to reflect on how successful he/she has been in fulfilling the expectations in the job description.

For teachers who hold allowances for specific tasks within a school, it is necessary to define clearly what is expected of them if they are to be successful, to whom and for whom they are accountable and the limits of delegated responsibility relating to budget and policy.

Below are examples of the job descriptions of a curriculum coordinator in a middle school and a head of department in a high school. Each document is an attempt to provide a written account of the job and its component tasks. The final example is a proforma intended to detail the job descriptions of teachers in a primary school.

EXAMPLE 14: JOB DESCRIPTION - MIDDLE SCHOOL CURRICULUM COORDINATOR

In consultation with the Headteacher, the Curriculum Coordinator is responsible for:

Curriculum Management

1. *Identifying overall aims and objectives in the subject.*
2. *Designing a curriculum within the subject relevant to the abilities and needs of pupils.*
3. *Organising curricular activities across the school and liaising with feeder first schools and receiving high schools.*
4. *Evaluating standards of learning.*
5. *Gathering and presenting information on pupil achievement.*
6. *Allocating the resources necessary for implementing the curriculum.*

Staff/Pupil Management

1. *Encouraging staff development and support within the curriculum area.*
2. *Motivating pupils and staff by personal influence and concern for individuals.*
3. *Helping to solve problems and resolve conflict by using skills of arbitration, negotiation and reconciliation.*
4. *Helping to establish effective channels of communication within the school.*

External Accountability

1. *Involving parents in school activities connected with the curriculum area as well as methods of working.*
2. *Reporting to parents, governors, advisory teachers and inspectors on overall policy and general standards of performance.*
3. *Helping to present the school to the local community through displays and exhibitions of work.*
4. *Liaising with other schools, industry and other groups for the benefit of the school, staff and pupils.*

EXAMPLE 15: JOB DESCRIPTION - HIGH SCHOOL HEAD OF DEPARTMENT

a. *To be responsible directly to the senior management for all matters relating to the running of the department.*
b. *To oversee the preparation of programmes of work, ordering of materials etc. - in consultation where appropriate.*
c. *To prepare programmes of work for new entrants and student teachers and to oversee their work within the department.*
d. *To ensure that the policy of the school is understood and carried out by members of the department.*
e. *To take responsibility for disciplinary matters referred by members of their team of staff and where necessary consulting with the appropriate head of year.*
f. *To be a member of the Steering Group and attend meetings as scheduled in directed time.*
g. *To control, monitor and supervise such records as are required by law or by the school.*
h. *To identify in-service training needs of the team as a whole and of its individual members.*
i. *To be prepared to initiate new ideas, to introduce new materials in the interests of improved efficiency and effectiveness.*
j. *To moderate course work in connection with examinations, records of achievement, etc for the department.*

38

EXAMPLE 16: JOB DESCRIPTION - PRIMARY SCHOOL TEACHER

JOB DESCRIPTION PRIMARY SCHOOL

PART 1

GENERAL   *You are required to carry out the duties of a school teacher as set out in School Teachers Pay and Conditions Document.*

PART II

1.   *NAME...*
2.   *POST...*
3.   *SALARY POINT............MAIN SCALE   PAY REF NO......................*
4.   *QUALIFICATIONS (date and subjects)*

    ...
    ...
    ...
    ...
    ...

5.   *DATE RECOGNISED AS QUALIFIED TEACHER...*
6.   *DATE APPOINTED TO SCHOOL...*
7.   *RELATIONSHIPS - The post holder is responsible to the Headteacher*
8.   *PURPOSE OF JOB - To undertake the teaching and planning of the curriculum, record keeping and assessment, pastoral and administrative duties in respect of pupils in CLASS .... YEAR GROUP..................*
9.   *SPECIFIC DUTIES*

    ...
    ...
    ...
    ...

PART III

10.   *In addition, you are required to undertake the responsibilities for which you are being paid an allowance as follows;*

    ...
    ...
    ...
    ...

11.   *The job description allocates duties and responsibilities. It does not direct the particular amount of time to spend in carrying them out and no part of it may be constructed. In allocating time to the performance of duties and responsibilities, the post holder, must use directed time in accordance with the school's policy, and have regard to clause 36 (1) of a Teacher's Conditions of Employment.*

12.   *The job description is not necessarily a comprehensive definition of the post and the teacher may be required to undertake such other tasks appropriate to the level of appointment as the headteacher may require. It may be reviewed annually or earlier if necessary and it may be subject to modification or amendment after consultation with the post holder.*

Signed (issued by): ....   *Date.................*
Signed (received by): ....   *Date.................*

The school needs to ensure that the job description is phrased in terms that are measurable at the point of any discussion or review with the post-holder. For example, it should be possible to take each of the job descriptors, frame it as a question, so that a range of success criteria could be discussed between appraiser and appraisee.

In the middle school example above, a discussion between appraisee and appraiser might explore point 3, as follows:

Appraiser: *"In your role as English coordinator, to what extent do you feel you have been able to organise curricular activities across the school and liaise with feeder schools?"*

Appraisee: *"Well, I think I've managed all the criteria raised by this point in my job description and if you wanted examples then I've arranged a subject evening for parents in the Autumn Term, I coordinated the Book Week activities across the school and, of course, I arrange the twice-termly liaison meeting with our feeder schools. I also attend the termly meetings with the high school. I feel that my next task should be to get a meeting between my staff with those that teach English in the high school to look at continuity at Key Stage 3. As you can imagine, this could have implications for teacher release. I have to say that I think this should be happening in all subjects, and I wouldn't mind taking responsibility for setting up a working party of other coordinators to look at the issues from this school's point of view."*

In summary, job descriptions should:

- be jointly discussed
- cover all aspects of a teacher's work
- specify to whom the teacher is accountable
- identify specific responsibilities
- be open-ended and capable of development
- enable the teacher to set priorities
- enable the teacher to set short term and long term targets
- be concise and straightforward
- be clear statements of what the teacher is expected to do
- be available to those other teachers entitled to see them.

Discussion about the nature of a teacher's work will have implications for many other aspects of the school. The appraiser needs to have insight into the appraisee's job and also the way in which it impinges upon the roles and responsibilities of others. The selection of appraiser for teachers is now considered.

Selection of Appraisers: Teachers

CIRCULAR 12/91: THE SELECTION OF APPRAISERS: SCHOOL TEACHERS (INCLUDING DEPUTY HEADS)

para.

21. Wherever possible the appraiser should already have management responsibility for the school teacher. In view of the responsibilities associated with the role of appraiser, appraisers should, in most circumstances, be responsible for no more than about 4 appraisees. Where, as a result of applying these guidelines, a school teacher will not be appraised by a person who already has management responsibility for him or her, the head teacher should appoint as appraiser a person who is in a position, by virtue of his or her experience and professional standing to ensure that the appraisal serves the needs of both the school teacher and the school.

22. It is the head teacher's responsibility to select the appraisers of school teachers in his or her school. However, head teachers should not refuse requests from staff for an alternative appraiser if there are particular circumstances which suggest that this might be appropriate. Such circumstances are likely to be exceptional.

It is the headteacher's responsibility to select the appraisers of teachers in his or her school. A limit of four appraisees per appraiser is sensible in most circumstances. If possible the appraiser should already have management responsibility for the teacher - otherwise it should be another teacher, who can meet the needs of both the appraisee and the school. In exceptional circumstances a teacher who has a valid reason to object to the appraiser appointed should be allowed an alternative.

In the interests of successful appraisal, appraisers should be selected with great sensitivity, matching personalities as far as possible and having regard to line management responsibilities. It is highly likely that most schools, particularly in the early stages of appraisal, will opt for a conventional line-management or hierarchical approach to appraisal as shown below:

HEADTEACHER

appraises

DEPUTY HEADTEACHER(S)

appraises

HEADS OF DEPARTMENT/FACULTY/YEAR/HOUSE/AREA

appraise

OTHER STAFF

It is by no means the only option available to schools, and the example below gives the structure adopted by one high school.

EXAMPLE 17: SELECTION OF APPRAISERS - HIGH SCHOOL MODEL

WHO WILL CONDUCT APPRAISAL?

The appraiser will normally have management responsibility for the appraisee. The Headteacher will notify each colleague, in confidence, of the arrangements before notifying their appraiser. He will be sympathetic to problems of "match" but any changes will have to be exceptional.

Responsibility for appraisal rests with the Heads of Faculty who will themselves be appraised on how well the system is operating in their areas by the Deputy Headteacher (Development).

In order to ensure that a manageable number of appraisals are undertaken by the Head of Faculty, use can be made of members of the Senior Management Team and/or Second in the Faculty or in some Faculties - such as Science, Technology, Humanities - Heads of Subject can be used, e.g. Physics, History, Home Economics.

Care will be taken by Heads of Faculty in allocating appraisers to ensure, where possible, an appropriate match of background knowledge, philosophy.

It is recognised that occasionally there may be good reason why an individual does not wish to be appraised by the person nominated. In such cases an individual should discuss the matter with the Headteacher or the Deputy Headteacher (Development). It is anticipated that such occasions will be rare.

Selection of Appraisers: Deputy Heads

CIRCULAR 12/91: THE SELECTION OF APPRAISERS: DEPUTY HEADS
para.
30. Deputy heads are covered by the arrangements for the selection of appraisers in respect of school teachers, except for the special provision in Regulation 8(6). This permits, but does not require, the head teacher to appoint two appraisers where that is considered appropriate by the appraising body. The head teacher will normally be one of the appraisers. Where the appraising body wishes deputy heads to have two appraisers, head teachers of voluntary aided schools should consult the governing body about the selection of the second appraiser.

Deputy headteachers have different conditions of service from other teachers, and their responsibilities, particularly in the secondary sector, are largely managerial. Because of the complex nature of the deputy's role, there is a strong case therefore for their appraisal to be more in line with headteacher appraisal than teacher appraisal, and for their appraisal to focus predominantly on the managerial aspects of their work. For that reason, appraising bodies have discretion to provide two appraisers for a deputy head. It is highly likely, and invariably desirable, that one of the appraisers will be the headteacher. The second appraiser could be an officer of the LEA, another deputy from within the same school or from another school, a colleague on the staff acceptable to the appraisee and who is in a position to provide meaningful feedback on an aspect of the deputys role. It may also be appropriate to make use of a member of an external agency such as the Careers Service for the purpose.

CHAPTER FIVE

The Appraisal Cycle: Headteachers

It is understandable that the broad principles set out for teachers within the Regulations and Circular 12/91 should also apply to headteachers, since there are features of the appraisal process which are common both to headteachers and teachers. They include the following:

- the process should be beneficial to the individual

- preparatory work should ensure a shared understanding of the aims and purposes of the LEA scheme. (Pilot studies pointed to the climate of trust and confidence between schools and LEAs which is necessary for the successful implementation of the scheme)

- training for both appraisers and appraisees is an essential part of the scheme

- agreement needs to be reached on the constituent parts of the actual process

- follow-up and review are essential to an effective appraisal process

It is equally understandable that the process of appraisal as it applies to headteachers will differ in practical terms from that of teachers by:

- the inclusion of an appraiser external to the school

- the necessity to distinguish between the appraisal of the headteacher and the appraisal of the institution

- the option to appraise either task or teaching and the consequent need to consider the nature of the task to be observed

- the ways in which support may be provided for achieving the targets which are set

The uniqueness of the headteacher's role has been the subject of several reports and commentaries (Hughes, 1976; Morgan, Hall and Mackay, 1983; Gane, 1986; West, 1990). In the particular context of appraisal the following items will require consideration:

- a head has no easily identifiable line manager

- a head has a complex role involving a wide range of shared and devolved responsibilities

- a head primarily manages others

- a head is isolated

- a head is wholly accountable to the governing body

The professional isolation of headteachers in general makes appraisal a vital issue. It is crucial that headteacher appraisal is carried out with rigour, yet with sensitivity. Approaches to headteacher appraisal have been many and varied, each with its own particular strengths and weaknesses.

The remainder of this chapter looks at the cycle as it applies specifically to headteachers.

Selecting the appraisers of headteachers

CIRCULAR 12/91: SELECTION OF APPRAISERS: HEAD TEACHERS
para.

23. It is recommended that LEAs delegate decisions on the selection of the appraisers of head teachers in schools they maintain to the Chief Education Officer (CEO). LEAs may wish to consider whether the CEO should have some guidelines, approved by the LEA, to assist in the exercise of this responsibility. The Regulations provide for the governing body to be responsible for selecting the appraisers of head teachers of grant-maintained schools.

24. The requirements in Regulation 8(4) have implications for the selection of the appraisers of head teachers of middle schools and nursery schools. Middle schools are formally designated as either primary or secondary schools: Regulation 8(4)(a) or 8(4)(b) will therefore apply as appropriate. However it is recommended that where the appraisee is the head teacher of a middle school, the appraiser appointed under Regulation 8(4) should, wherever possible, also be the head teacher of a middle school. Nursery schools are formally designated as primary schools: the selection of appraisers for the head teachers of such schools will therefore fall under Regulation 8(4)(a). However it is recommended that where the appraisee is the head teacher of a nursery school, the appraiser appointed under Regulation 8(4)(a) should, wherever possible, have experience of early childhood education.

25. In the case of county, voluntary controlled, voluntary aided, special agreement and maintained special schools, one of the two appraisers should normally be an officer or adviser of the LEA. Both appraisers should normally be present at both the initial meeting and the appraisal interview. Regulation 9(3) allows observation of the appraisee in the classroom or performing other duties to be undertaken by either one or both of the appraisers. If only one of the appraisers is involved in this observation, it is recommended that this appraiser should be the one who has relevant experience as a head teacher under Regulation 8(4).

26. Governing bodies of denominational voluntary aided schools are advised to consult the relevant diocese about the selection of the appraiser who is not an LEA officer.

27. In the case of special agreement schools in which the head teacher has reserved teacher status, it is recommended that the LEA should consult the governing body about the selection of appraisers.

28. Head teachers should not be able to choose their appraisers but great care should be taken in the matching of appraisers with appraisees. Requests from appraisees for alternative appraisers should not be refused where the circumstances suggest that they might be appropriate, for example, where the interests of an appraising head's school may be in conflict with those of the appraisee's school.

29. Serving head teachers should not be required to act as appraiser for more than three other head teachers at a time.

The approach endorsed by the Government in its Regulations and in Circular 12/91 requires that LEAs appoint two appraisers for the headteachers of county, voluntary controlled, voluntary aided, special agreement and maintained special schools, after consulting the governing body. One of these should be a headteacher from the same phase and/or type of school as the appraisee, and the other a representative from the LEA. (For grant-maintained schools it is the governing body that appoints the two appraisers.) If this approach is used, one method of pairing is to consider the following strategy:

- the appraising body groups the heads into 4s or 5s according to negotiated and agreed criteria such as comparative size of school, presence of 6th Form, denomination, element of local competition.
- each head is offered the opportunity to express one negative preference from the names proposed
- the appraising body acts as "honest broker" in allocating matching pairs

The second appraiser - "an officer or adviser of the LEA" - offers the scheme credibility and an element of support to heads in their management development.

Some LEAs may choose to use groups of seconded headteachers for this purpose. They do so by identifying, from among practising headteachers in the different phases of education, a cohort who would be offered secondment for a specified period to act as headteacher appraisers. Alternatively, an LEA may identify a substantial number of headteachers who would be allowed additional staffing for the time involved in appraisal activity.

Both appraisers will need to be familiar with current national and local policies about curriculum, special needs, equal opportunities, disciplinary and grievance procedures and similar issues affecting management. In addition they will need to familiarise themselves with the circumstances of the school in question. Some notion of the context and the manner in which the school functions can be gleaned from the school's development plan, the staff handbook and information prepared for parents such as the school prospectus and newsletters.

Broadly speaking, headteacher appraisal has the same components as described for teachers, although it is likely to have a wider context.

Initial meeting

This serves similar purposes to those listed for teachers, but the meeting is mandatory in the case of heads. The meeting should aim to:

- help the headteacher and his/her appraisers consider the school's current situation and the appraisee's thoughts regarding his/her position;
- help the headteacher take stock of his/her role;
- help the headteacher reflect upon his/her performance of the role in global terms;
- help the headteacher's appraisers familiarise themselves with the school, the role of the headteacher and the possible focus of the appraisal process;
- provide the opportunity for both parties to agree the focus for the appraisal cycle;
- clarify the nature and extent of the data needed to support the appraisal process.

Self-appraisal

Although the scope of this may be limited by focuses decided at the initial meeting, it is nevertheless taxing and time-consuming. Yet, headteachers who are prepared to undertake some form of self-appraisal and then to share their thoughts and feelings with the appraisers, can derive considerable benefit from the process. The use of appropriate proformas as shown below can assist this process by offering some kind of structure for recording thoughts, ideas, concerns.

EXAMPLE 18: HEADTEACHER SELF-APPRAISAL PROFORMA *FOCUS: Relationships*
Pupils
Staff (including support staff)
Governors
Parents
Community
LEA
Administration

46

EXAMPLE 19: HEADTEACHER SELF-APPRAISAL PROFORMA

1.	*JOB DESCRIPTION* *Is it fully relevant? What needs to be amended?*

2.	*ACHIEVEMENTS AND EFFECTIVENESS* *With which aspects of your job do you feel especially pleased?* *Which aspects of your job have not gone as well as you hoped?*

3.	*CONSTRAINTS* *Have you encountered any constraints in trying to do your job?* *How might the way your job is organised/managed be improved?*

4.	*THE FUTURE* *What training/development needs do you foresee for the next year or so to help you do your job better?* *What further experience would you want to help you do your job better?* *Are your abilities, knowledge, skills being used to the full either within your school or your LEA?*

5.	*CAREER DEVELOPMENT* *Do you have aspirations for the future? What are they?*

6.	*OTHER POINTS*

(adapted from *Managing Appraisal*, Secondary Heads Association)

Classroom observation

At least one observer should see the head teaching or carrying out other duties on at least two occasions. If the head has a regular teaching responsibility, classroom observation is normally appropriate but, particularly if the teaching commitment is small or infrequent, task observation may take its place entirely or in part. If only one observer does this, it should be the one who has relevant experience as a head teacher.

Task observation

The issue of task observation is one which raises particular concerns, especially in relation to time, relevance and the nature and scope of the data collection methods. The two case-studies that follow are intended to highlight the implications of such an approach. They each describe the process from pre-appraisal meetings where the manageable focus of the appraisal was decided, through the process of data collection, to the final professional discussion with the headteacher, and a summary of targets. The overall conclusion section draws together the factors which need to be considered in drawing up a programme of headteacher task appraisal.

CASE-STUDY 1

The task focus was chosen by the Headteacher - the system of appraisal which she had introduced in a primary school of 12 staff.

The preliminary meeting with the two appraisers, a headteacher from the same phase of education and the "patch" inspector, established that they would observe the Headteacher during one day conducting a classroom observation, a review of target setting, and a staff development interview.

The whole staff were made aware of the scope and nature of the activity and the three members of staff specifically concerned had further consultations with the Headteacher to reassure them that the exercise was one of appraisal of the Headteacher and not of them.

When the appraisers arrived at the school they were given the timetable which included space for meeting the three teachers, and other staff as debriefing time for the Headteacher. A supply teacher was available to release the staff from their commitments as necessary.

The appraisers met the Headteacher at 8.55am and went through the programme. She explained that it was the first time that she had included classroom observation in the scheme and gave them copies of the schedule that she was using. She also provided a copy of the review on which target setting was based. There was no copy of the self-appraisal sheet for the staff development interview. She explained that she had nominated the three members of staff for particular reasons:

A.   was nominated for classroom observation because she was in charge of the reception class, a key role. She was perceived to be positive in her approach to school and to the changes which the Headteacher, in her second year of Headship had brought about.

B.   was the Deputy Head, who would be involved as an appraiser when the scheme was fully introduced. It would therefore be useful experience for him to be involved in the exercise.

C.   was a teacher whose self-development interview was due and who was also willing for external appraisers to be present.

<u>Data Collection</u>

The appraisers then saw the three members of staff together to explain the purpose of the day and the procedures that would be adopted, to reassure them that the Headteacher was undergoing appraisal and to confirm the confidentiality aspects of the exercise.

The classroom observation was then discussed with A. The schedule was a form of lesson plan which she had completed and then photocopied for the Headteacher. A seemed unsure about what was to be appraised. There had been no preliminary discussion to negotiate a focus and she was unsure how to complete Part 2 of the schedule, a consideration of how she had met the objectives of her plan and what would happen as a result of the classroom observation. She approved of the inclusion of classroom observation in the scheme and did not think that 2 x 30 minutes periods were unrealistic. The Headteacher was often in classrooms, actively involved in lessons and therefore would know if a teacher was acting outside her usual pattern. She acknowledged that in some schools such confidence would not be possible.

The classroom observation lasted for 30 minutes. The teacher reminded the children of the work which they had done on the letter "d" and then they were put into three groups with tasks to reinforce their learning. A parent helper was present to support her. The appraisers sat in a position where it was possible to view the Headteacher and all of the class activities.

Following the lesson, one of the appraisers had a brief discussion with A about her reaction to the exercise, while the second appraiser returned to the office with the Headteacher to discuss her reactions.

The review and target-setting exercise with the Deputy Head began with the updating of his job description as it related to the targets set at his staff development interview six months earlier. Only the Headteacher had a copy. Appropriate training for new tasks was discussed and how success might be measured. The Deputy Head had prepared his list of targets under the separate headings of "Management" and "Classroom" Teaching. The Headteacher picked up possibilities for developing his role as Deputy Head and the discussion widened into the relationship between the School Development Plan and In-service Training provision. Finally the targets were prioritised and a further review arranged in three months time. The Headteacher wrote down the agreed targets and the support needed and promised to provide a neat copy the next day. The interview lasted for 30 minutes.

The staff development interview for C was based on the post for which she was receiving an allowance. The teacher worked through a prepared self-evaluation schedule. Neither the appraisers nor the Headteacher had a copy. There was a sharing of philosophies and strategies which led to target setting. The Headteacher made notes under headings and promised a neat draft of the agreed targets the next day. The interview lasted for one hour.

The appraisers then decided to see B and C individually to test their reactions to the exercise.

The Deputy Head was satisfied with the interview. He felt that he had gained what he wanted and felt that he would have the support necessary for him to reach his targets. He was not distracted by the Headteacher writing during the interview and felt that 30 minutes was adequate as he had regular consultations with her. He did not feel disadvantaged by not having a copy of his previous interview and was unsure whether he had seen it and signed it. However, he was aware of the on-going nature of the appraisal scheme.

C was doubtful about the value of the exercise. When prompted she said that she did feel encouraged and was aware that the Headteacher was concerned that she should do well. She was less convinced that the support would be available for her to achieve her targets. She spoke of the time between the staff development interview and the review of targets as a "vacuum". She saw appraisal as "another change" and did not appreciate its on-going purpose. She did not like the emphasis on her management role as she saw herself primarily as a class teacher.

(Case Study 1 continued)

Over a working lunch the appraisers discussed the exercise with the Headteacher. Generally, she felt that the day had been tiring because normally the three activities would have taken place on separate days. She had not been happy with the classroom observation for a variety of reasons. Usually she became involved in classroom activities and did not like sitting in one place. She also found the schedule she had adopted too narrow.

The targets review with the Deputy Head had become more of a target setting exercise and she agreed with the appraisers that the Deputy Head had set the agenda and directed the discussion.

The staff development interview with C went much as she had expected. Again she was able to provide the background to the interview which explained her approach. She wondered if the target setting had been realistic in view of the time which she would need to commit to supporting the teacher.

The appraisers left the school at 3.00 pm and later sent their recommendation to the Headteacher.

Recommendations

The observations which were later communicated to the Headteacher by the appraisers took the form of recommendations which might help her to support areas which she had agreed in discussion needed development.

1. *The need for pre-activity discussions to establish the agenda.*
2. *The need for a whole school discussion to establish what staff perceive as good classroom practice.*
3. *The need for negotiation of the focus of appraisal in the classroom. One which would enable the Headteacher to interact comfortably as appraiser with the Headteacher and the children. The appraisers suggested that a relevant focus might be - the use of parent helpers; the organisation of groups; the monitoring of particular children.*
4. *Discussion with the staff of the purpose of appraisal in terms of professional discussion between appraiser and appraisee. This related back to the negotiation of focus.*
5. *The value of the appraisee having photocopies of self-evaluation sheets in order to prepare for staff development interviews. Discussion can be consequently more structured and the appraiser can prepare for issues which may be raised.*
6. *Consideration of the time which is demanded of the appraiser in order to support the achievement of targets. In the case of C, the appraisers suggested that the Headteacher set aside half an hour each month for a discussion. This strategy might ease C's need for regular reassurance.*
7. *Discussion with staff on how realistic the exercise in target setting was in relation to the school development plan and the school budget.*
8. *The importance of the cycle of appraisal to be discussed with staff.*
9. *Discussion with the staff of how the appraisal of a management role and that of the classroom teacher might be conducted.*

CASE STUDY 2

The task focus was chosen by the Headteacher at a preliminary discussion with the appraisers. The appraisee, a Headteacher of a Middle School, requested that the appraisers observe him during an open morning specifically for new children shortly to arrive from the neighbouring First Schools. Their parents had also been invited. In addition members of the Governing Body would be present. The appraisers joined the Headteacher at 8.30am prior to the meeting.

The Headteacher's aims were:

1. *To provide information visually and verbally about the school.*
2. *To enable new children to experience the view of school life in all its aspects.*
3. *To project himself to the parents in a positive light as the "leader" i.e. marketing the school through himself.*

Data Collection

Initially, parents and children were ushered into the school hall where they waited for a few minutes while the Headteacher waited for latecomers. He then addressed them for about fifteen minutes - introducing himself and the various school booklets he wished to distribute. 28 children and 18 adults were present, but 4 other adults (including the Chair of Governors and a Parent Governor) arrived during the course of the morning.

After a brief introduction he invited them to follow him around the school to see other children and the teachers at work. Apart from the formal "chat", the Head was able to talk informally with some parents and children.

He talked to the parents, stressing the similarity of the classes in resources, etc. and encouraging the children to sample some of the lessons and the activities taking place. Throughout, the Headteacher was responding to questions asked by parents and children.

During the "walk about" the Headteacher was explaining the different areas of the school and introducing various classes and teachers including the Deputy Head. During this time he was able to continue to talk informally with new parents and children and the appraisers. A break of about 25 minutes was taken when some children went to the playground and parents were offered coffee. Parents could then collect the school brochure and mix informally with each other.

The appraisers received a copy of the original letter to parents inviting them to school, and studied the school brochure and attached notes for guidance. During the morning the appraisers talked to a range of staff, a Parent Governor, the Chair of Governors, the Deputy Head. The appraisers concentrated on the stated aims of the morning and discovered:

- *great satisfaction with the view the new entrants had received of the school;*
- *pleasure with the way the new entries had reacted to the school;*
- *much satisfaction with the performance of the Headteacher. He was appointed two years ago and was perceived as energetic, professional and friendly. His aim of projecting a positive image of himself would seem to be meeting with some success. The Chairman had been especially complimentary as he felt it justified his recommendation of the original appointment.*

Recommendations

The appraisers discussed the morning with the Headteacher and later made the following written recommendations:

1. *Consideration of the "audience" for this meeting. At times he varied his tone and the content of his talk to speak to children and then to parents.*
2. *The need to consider this meeting within the whole induction process, in order to clarify the organisation.*
3 *A reconsideration of the tour of the school in terms of the large number of parents plus children. At times it was difficult for those at the back of the group to hear what was being said. The appraisers asked if the inclusion of the Deputy Head might help the organisation. There seemed to be a particular difficulty in coping with latecomers.*

At least three important issues arose from the case studies:

• *Task observation within the appraisal process needs to be manageable for both appraisers and Headteachers in terms of the time invested.*
• *The exercise should be meaningful and the recommendations should be made on valid and reliable data.*
• *All staff should be informed of the existence of the exercise and its purpose.*

Collection of information

The range of possible sources of information is wider than for teachers - staff governors, parents and LEA officers. Appraisees should be consulted about the sources and methods of collection. Information collection, in respect of headteachers, should normally be completed within one term. The following sources of information are likely to be of some help to appraisers:

• **publicly or professionally available data relating to the working of the school**.
  It is important to restrict this process to manageable proportions since it is highly unlikely that appraisers will be able to read everything that is offered to them. Appraisers can be provided with the background information they need via the staff handbook, parents' newsletters, 6th Form prospectus, curriculum guides, annual report to governors and parents, examination/test results, etc.

• **task and/or classroom observation**
  Except in the case of headteachers of some primary schools who have a full or substantial teaching commitment, it is unlikely that headteachers will wish to be observed at work in the classroom. This should not preclude any headteacher who sincerely wishes to have feedback on his/her performance within the classroom from being offered the opportunity. Other headteachers may wish to do so in order to "lead by example" and/or to demonstrate to staff credibility as a practitioner.

• **interviews with staff, governors, parents, etc**
  brief, structured and relevant discussions with appropriate members of the staff, members of the governing body as well as parents, may offer valuable objective feedback.

- **consultation with LEA officers including inspectors**
  LEA officers and inspectors have useful information and insights in respect of the schools for which they are responsible. Most LEAs have a programme of regular reviews of their schools, as well as a link or "patch" inspector. This data can be useful in guiding headteachers when selecting their focus area(s) and in offering feedback during the appraisal discussion stage.

As with teachers, headteachers should be familiar with any guidance or codes of practice offered nationally or locally in respect of the collection of information to support appraisal. An example of such guidance is shown below:

EXAMPLE 20: CODE OF PRACTICE FOR THE COLLECTION OF INFORMATION FOR HEADTEACHER APPRAISAL

This code of practice covers the collection of information for appraisal other than through classroom observation.

General principles

1. *The appraisers should agree with the appraisee at the initial meeting what information it would be appropriate to collect for the purpose of the appraisal, from what sources and by what methods. Appraisers are not expected to consult parents, pupils or governors about an appraisee unless the information sought has direct relevance to the aspect of work being appraised.*
2. *Any written submission should remain confidential to the author, the appraiser and the appraisee.*
3. *The collection of information for the purpose of appraisal should be designed to support discussion in an appraisal interview.*
4. *Where it has been agreed that the appraisal should concentrate on specific aspects of the appraisee's job, the collection of information should concentrate on the same specific aspects.*
5. *Appraisers should act with sensitivity to all concerned and should not exhibit any bias in the collection of information.*
6. *Providers of information should not be put under any pressure save that of relevance and accuracy.*
7. *Comments of a general nature should be supported by specific examples.*
8. *Interviews for the purpose of information collection should be held on a one to one basis.*
9. *Any information received anonymously should be ignored and destroyed.*
10. *Information which does not relate to the professional performance of a teacher should not be sought or accepted.*
11. *Appraisees should not adopt an obstructive attitude to reasonable proposals for the collection of appropriate information.*
12. *Neither appraisers nor appraisees should act in any way that is likely to threaten the trust and confidence on both sides upon which successful appraisal depends.*
13. *When interviewing people providing information as part of an appraisal, the appraiser should attempt to explain the purpose of the interview and the way in which information will be treated.*
14. *Those giving information should be encouraged to make fair and constructive comments which they are prepared to acknowledge and to substantiate if required.*
15. *Those offering significantly critical comments should be asked to discuss them directly with the appraisee before they are used as appraisal information. (The substance of grievance or disciplinary proceedings should never be used in the appraisal process).*
16. *Except where personal opinion is specifically sought (for example, where an appraiser is attempting to gauge staff reactions to a particular innovation), care should be taken to ensure that information is sought and presented in an objective way.*

Appraisal interview

The interview or professional discussion is likely to be similar in purpose to that of the teacher appraisal interview, including target setting. However, since both appraisers are expected to be present at the head's interview, it is important that both have come to some agreement about their strategy for conducting the interview, how the various stages will be handled, who will lead the discussion, and who will keep note of the discussion. If only one of the appraisers is likely to be present at the interview, it is desirable that he/she should be the one with relevant experience of headship.

Appraisal statements

Preparation of the head's appraisal statement has the same conditions as for teachers, except that there are two appraisers involved.

In the event of complaint by the head, then two review officers will be required (appointed by the appraising body). In the case of voluntary aided schools, the County Education Officer and the governing body have to agree, failing which they appoint one review officer each. If a new appraisal is ordered, the criteria governing the original appointment of the appraisers and the general conduct of the appraisal, apply.

Use and retention of appraisal records

The appraisers are required to provide a copy of the statement to:

(i)   the CEO (or a specifically designated officer), if the school is maintained by the LEA; and
(ii)   the chair of the governors in all cases

Follow up: the review meeting

This is an important element of the appraisal process and although much of the follow-up will take place informally, by telephone or by asking for a brief get-together, there is still a need to formalise the procedure in order to comply with the requirements of the DfE scheme. In doing so the appraiser has the opportunity of exploring with the appraisee the way in which progress is being made in relation to the previously agreed goals. The appraisee, in turn, can use the opportunity to mention constraints, to request specific assistance including resources, to consider further training needs that may have arisen, etc.

As with teacher appraisal the job description can provide a useful focus for the headteacher appraisal interview. An example is shown below:

EXAMPLE 21: HEADTEACHER JOB DESCRIPTION

To assume responsibility for the internal organisation and management of the School and to exercise supervision over teaching and non-teaching staff;

To determine, organise and ensure the implementation of the secular curriculum; and

To regulate the conduct of the pupils.

SPECIFIC DUTIES

a)   *The Organisation and Management of the School*

determining the internal policies of the school;
communicating with parents and others;
establishing a staffing structure, appointing staff, deploying and managing staff;
stimulating and supporting the professional development of staff;
managing all financial resources;
supervising the maintenance and security of equipment and accommodation;
maintaining appropriate educational and administrative records;
establishing clear policies on the maintenance of order and discipline;
maintaining relationships with organisations representing staff.

b)   *identifying the aims and objectives which will be the basis of the school curriculum;*
translating aims and objectives into a curriculum relevant to the abilities, aptitudes and needs of all pupils and ensuring that there are schemes of work for all sections or departments in the school and monitoring their implementation;
establishing a system and programme for pupil guidance, counselling and pastoral care;
maintaining appropriate records of pupil performance;
in consultation with staff, developing appropriate criteria for the evaluation of the effectiveness of both teaching and learning and using results to initiate necessary improvement;
participating in the teaching of pupils.

c)   *Accountability*

attending and reporting to Governors' meetings
taking note of Governors' views when shaping School policies;
liaison with the Chairman of Governors;
implementing the policies of the LEA

d)   *External Relations*

liaison with feeder Schools and those institutions to which pupils may transfer;
constructively involving parents in the life and work of the School;
representing the School to other groups in the local community and to the media;
liaison with support agencies;
working closely with LEA.

CHAPTER SIX

Components of the Appraisal Cycle (1)

Appraisal cannot be regarded as a set of techniques or a discrete process with an easily definable boundary. The principles and practice of appraisal are inextricably linked to the management process in any organisation, and to that organisation's philosophy towards people.

CIRCULAR 12/91: METHODS
para.
31.   Appraisal involves the evaluation of the professional performance of an appraisee by the appraisee and an appraiser together, and the establishment of targets for future action and development. The components of appraisal for school teachers and head teachers respectively are set out below: together they constitute a single appraisal programme.

This chapter deals with the initial meeting, self-appraisal, classroom observation and task observation.

CIRCULAR 12/91: SCHOOL TEACHERS
para.
32.   The components of appraisal for school teachers should be as follows:
- classroom observation;
- an appraisal interview, in which targets for action are established;
- the preparation of an appraisal statement;
- follow up, including a review meeting between the appraiser and appraisee.
The process may also include an initial meeting between the appraiser and the appraisee, self-appraisal by the appraisee and, after consultation with the appraisee, collection of data from sources other than classroom observation.

Initial Meeting

CIRCULAR 12/91: THE INITIAL MEETING
para.
33.   It may be helpful for appraisal to begin with a meeting between the appraisee and the appraiser to plan and prepare for the appraisal, particularly if the appraiser is unfamiliar with the appraisee's post.

Though left as an option in the appraisal of teachers there seems a general recognition in schools that an initial meeting is of great importance. For example, it is important that both the appraiser and the appraisee take the opportunity to clarify both the purpose of appraisal and the elements of the appraisal cycle in order to reach shared understanding. In more specific terms, the meeting should:

•   confirm the purpose and clarify the context of the appraisal;

- consider the teacher's agreed areas of responsibility;
- agree the scope of the appraisal, identifying areas of the appraisee's job on which the appraisal might usefully focus;
- agree arrangements for classroom observation;
- agree on the methods other than classroom observation by which data for the appraisal should be collected, and from whom;
- agree a time-table for the conduct of the appraisal.

Getting off to a good start is crucial and the initial meeting has an important part to play in establishing a climate which is conducive to appraisal. Preparation for this meeting should be thorough if the appraiser and appraisee are going to have an informed, professional discussion. The appraisee should come to the meeting:

- having reflected on a possible focus for classroom observation and, if appropriate, task observation

- having considered a possible strategy for the gathering of data/information to support the observation

- with a copy of his/her time-table, job description, and any other papers or documents felt to be relevant

- prepared to take an active role in the meeting, knowing its purpose and willing to discuss frankly and honestly

- prepared to negotiate schedules for recording observations and for collecting information

- prepared to negotiate dates and times for the various elements of the cycle

Similarly, the appraiser should come to the meeting:

- having agreed time and venue with the appraisee (the appraisee might be invited to suggest a venue)

- having considered the appraisee's job description

- with a copy of both their own and the appraisee's time-table, job description, and of the school's arrangement for appraisal

- prepared to encourage the appraisee to take a leading role in the meeting and to negotiate the record to be made concerning the various elements of the cycle

Figure 6.1: APPRAISER AND APPRAISEE TASKS AT THE INITIAL MEETING

The appraisee's task in this meeting is:	The appraiser's task in this meeting is:
• to suggest possible foci for observation	• to listen to the appraisee's suggestions for possible foci for observation
• to assist in clarifying the nature and meaning of the foci	• to help the appraisee clarify the nature and meaning of the foci
• to agree where and when the observation will take place	• to encourage the appraisee to decide on how evidence might best be collected and recorded to provide the basis for a professional discussion
• to decide how evidence might best be collected and recorded to provide the basis for a professional discussion	• to agree the style of the observation i.e. the extent of appraiser participation, the seating arrangement, explaining the appraiser's presence to the pupils
• to agree the style of the observation i.e. the degree of appraiser involvement, seating arrangement, informing the pupils, etc	• to agree the information concerning the context of the observation to be provided for the appraiser by the appraisee i.e. the place of the activity in the teaching programme, the appraisee's aims for the lesson/task to be observed, the follow-up work planned
• to agree the information concerning the context of the observation to be provided for the appraiser by the appraisee i.e. the place of the activity in the teaching programme, the appraisee's aims for the lesson/task to be observed, the follow-up work planned	• to agree the time and place for informal feedback, and the records/information to be passed to the appraisee following observation
• to agree the time and place for informal feedback, the records/information to be passed to the appraisee following observation	• to agree the time-table for the various elements of the cycle
	• to agree the agenda for the appraisal interview

In summary it is important that at the end of the initial meeting both the appraiser and appraisee are agreed as to:

• the time-table for the process

• the exact procedure to be followed

• the observation schedule to be employed during the classroom visit

• the appraisal interview agenda

58

Example 22 below offers a proforma for use throughout the appraisal cycle; which offers a useful structure for discussion.

EXAMPLE 22: ARRANGEMENTS FOR APPRAISAL

Initial Meeting: Appraisee/Appraiser Confidential Record

Appraisee: _____   *Appraiser:* _____

Scope of the Appraisal: the areas to be considered

The Appraisal Interview Agenda

Methods of collecting and recording classroom observation data

Records/information to be provided for appraisee:

Date:

Task Observation/Data Collection from other sources

Task/Information sought:

Method(s) of collection:

Records/information to be provided for appraisee:

Date:

Classroom Observation

Group: *Room:*   *Date:*   *Lessons:*

Informal feedback date/time:

Information concerning context to be provided by appraisee for appraiser:

Date:

Classroom Observation

Group: *Room:*   *Date:*   *Lessons:*

Informal feedback date/time:

Information concerning context to be provided by appraisee for appraiser:

Date:

Appraisal Interview and Statement

Interview date:

Statement produced (copies to appraisee and appraiser)
Date: w/c   *(5 working days after interview)*

Statement agreed (signed by appraisee and appraiser):
Date: w/c   *(20 working days after statement produced)*

Signatures: Appraisee: _____

         Appraiser: _____

         Date: _____

Self-appraisal

> **CIRCULAR 12/91: SELF APPRAISAL**
> **para.**
> **34.** As part of their preparation for the appraisal, school teachers should be encouraged to recognise the value of self-appraisal and to carry it out. Self-appraisal is not compulsory. Where it is carried out it should inform all other aspects of the process, in particular the appraisal interview.

Self-review or self-appraisal remains an option within the government regulations for appraisal. Such a process is clearly a personal issue as well as a consideration for the institution, but it does offer appraisees an opportunity to reflect on their own performance.

> You can't develop people. That door is locked from the inside. You must create a climate in which people will develop themselves

Robert Townsend, *Up the Organisation*, 1970

> All personal development is self-development which happens when people use whatever opportunities are available to increase their skills, knowledge, their competence and confidence

John Harvey Jones, *Making it Happen*, 1989

Its purpose is to help appraisees get the maximum benefit from the appraisal programme. Self-review may be useful at various stages in the appraisal cycle:

- prior to the initial meeting to help clarify focus areas
- as preparation for the appraisal interview itself
- as preparation for classroom observation
- during/following classroom observation

Specifically, appraisee self-appraisal can help:

- ensure that appraisal is a two-way process
- ensure that the appraisee clarifies thoughts and knows what he or she wants from the process
- encourage on-going reflection to celebrate success and establish improvement

To be effective self-appraisal should:

- prompt reflection in a structured way
- cover appropriate aspects of the job
- include a view of how the job should be done
- give rise to reliable data
- establish a clear picture of performance
- not take a disproportionate amount of time
- provide information which is helpful
- accommodate the school's philosophy

Self-review may be recorded in various ways, ranging from the formal, structured means to one which is less structured. The important issue is that the process offers the opportunity for reflection. As with all appraisal documents, prompt sheets and pro-formas, they need to be considered carefully before they are adopted. Discussions will need to take place in order to reach decisions about the confidentiality aspect of self-appraisal. Are the completed proformas intended for the appraisee's eyes only? Should any sharing of the content of a self-appraisal proforma be left to the discretion of the appraisee alone? Current practice in schools points clearly to all self-review documents being treated in the strictest confidence, with documentation being shared with the appraiser prior to any discussion if felt to be appropriate by the appraisee.

Above all, they should suit the context of the school and be consistent with the approach to appraisal being developed. For example, if a school focus is decided upon for classroom observation, two types of forms, or two sections might be needed; one which relates specifically to a person's job, the other to the specific focus of the observation.

The development of a school review form can be an activity which encourages staff to consider the value of self-review and whether one all-purpose format or a variety of alternative types will suit their school and their appraisal process.

A range of possible self-review forms are set out below in an attempt to facilitate discussion between colleagues regarding a workable format:

EXAMPLE 23: SELF APPRAISAL FORMAT (1)

1.   *Which parts of your job do you enjoy and why?*

2.   *Which parts of your job do you like least and why?*

3.   *Do you have skills or abilities which you do not use in your job?*

4.   *Under what conditions do you work most effectively?*

5.   *Which are your key job skills?*

6.   *What other skills or knowledge do you feel would be useful?*

7.   *Are there any key training needs that emerge from your agreed targets?*

8.   *What additional education, training or experience do you think you need?*

EXAMPLE 24: SELF APPRAISAL FORMAT (2)

1.   *JOB DESCRIPTION*

      Set down a brief list of what you consider to be the key tasks and responsibilities of your job.

2.   *THE YEAR'S WORK*

      What have you done with greatest satisfaction?

      How could these aspects of your work be used to best advantage?

      What have you done with least satisfaction?

      What could be done to overcome these difficulties?

3.   *OBSTACLES*

      Were there any obstacles which hindered you from accomplishing what you wished?

      Are they likely to recur?

      If so, how could they be eliminated?

4.   *IMPROVEMENT*

      To make your job performance better, what additional things might be done by:

      a)   *your headteacher?*

      b)   *yourself?*

      c)   *anyone else?*

5.   *TARGETS FOR NEXT YEAR*

      What do you think should be the key aims in your targets for next year?

6.   *CAREER*

      What do you hope to be doing in, say 3 years time?

      How would you like to see your career developing?

EXAMPLE 25: SELF APPRAISAL FORMAT (3)

○   *What do you consider to be the main tasks and responsibilities of your current post?*

○   *During the past academic year, what aspects of your work have given you*
        -      *the greatest satisfaction?*
        -      *the least satisfaction?*

○   *Did anything prevent you from achieving something you had intended or hoped to do?*

○   *Have these obstacles been removed?*

○   *What in your view would be the main goals for the next year?*

○   *What help do you need to this end? and from whom?*

○   *How do you envisage your career developing?*

EXAMPLE 26: SELF APPRAISAL FORMAT (4)	High				Low
How do I rate my:	1	2	3	4	5
Organisation of work within my areas of responsibility					
Ability to lead colleagues, drawing together their ideas and developing good practice					
Ability to support, influence and develop the work of colleagues for whom I am responsible					
Work in liaising with colleagues in complementary roles in feeder and transfer schools					
Effectiveness in maintaining records for which I am responsible					
Work in liaising with teachers in related areas of responsibility					
Consideration of recent reports and developments in the areas for which I am responsible					
Effectiveness in keeping others informed about the work in my areas of responsibility					
Skills in counselling colleagues who need my help					
Skill in running meetings					

EXAMPLE 27: SELF APPRAISAL FORMAT (5)

Read through your job description.

CURRICULUM - OTHER RESPONSIBILITIES

1. *With which aspects of your job and work do you feel especially pleased?*

2. *Which aspects of your job have not gone as well as you had hoped?*

3. *Are you working under any constraints or difficulties?*

TEACHING RESPONSIBILITIES

4. *Are you happy with the age group you are teaching?*

5. *Read through the analysis of teaching schedule. In which area do you feel your strengths lie?*

6. *Choose two different sub-areas which you feel would benefit from further analysis. Decide what information/data you would like collected by your classroom observer which would throw light on these areas of teaching. Fill in the analysis of teaching form.*

STAFF DEVELOPMENT PROFILE

a. *Identify any achievements you would like added to your profile.*

b. *List all INSET/courses attended - qualifications gained in the last year.*

c. *What are your targets for next year with regard to your curriculum and other responsibilities.*

d. *Are there any ways in which you would like to develop your experience and strengthen your expertise in the coming 2 years?*

EXAMPLE 28: SELF APPRAISAL FORMAT (6)

AREAS FOR DISCUSSION:

JOB DESCRIPTION:

Are you clear about what it states?

Are there any amendments you wish to make?

AREAS OF SUCCESS:

Which aspect/areas of your role have pleased you this year?

DIFFICULTIES THAT HAVE OCCURRED:

What difficulties have arisen and what assistance might you need with respect to these?

AREAS FOR DEVELOPMENT:

Which areas of your role do you particularly wish to develop?

OBJECTIVES/TARGETS:

What objectives do you wish to achieve this year?

SUPPORT:

Is there any support you would welcome in either professional or personal development terms?

EXAMPLE 29: SELF APPRAISAL FORMAT (7)

Would you please complete the document and return it to me prior to our discussion meeting.

Date: *Time:*   *Place:*

SECTION 1

a)   *Name..*
b)   *Present post ....*
c)   *Date appointed to post ....*
d)   *Date appointed to school ....*
e)   *Major responsibilities that are additional to classroom teaching*
         ..
         ..

SECTION 2 - Personal Satisfaction

a)   *What is your general feeling/satisfaction with your present post/responsibilities?*

b)   *What is your general feeling/satisfaction with your present year group/classroom*

c)   *What is your general feeling/satisfaction with the level of pupil progress in*
         i)   *your areas of responsibility*
         ii)   *your class*

d)   *What developments would you want to see in*
         i)   *your areas of responsibility*
         ii)   *your classroom next year*

e)   *Which aspects of school do you see as working particularly well?*

SECTION 3 - INSET

a)   *What INSET have you been involved in during the last 12 months?*

b)   *Was it valuable to you?*
         Would it be valuable to others?

c)   *Are there any particular courses or other forms of support you would like in the near future (please consider funding implications)*
         i)   *in relation to your responsibilities?*
         ii)   *in relation to your classwork?*
         iii)   *for your personal career development?*

SECTION 4 - Curriculum

a)   *Is there any particular development need for your area of responsibility?*

b)   *In a more general way is there any particular <u>curriculum</u> area you think we should seek to develop?*

c)   *What do you see as the most pressing item for our next INSET day? (How could the day be organised?)*

Classroom Observation

Classroom observation is only one way of gathering data for appraisal purposes but if appraisal of performance is about improving the quality of children's education by improving teacher effectiveness, then looking at what actually happens within the classroom is vital.

CIRCULAR 12/91: CLASSROOM OBSERVATION

para.

35. School teachers should normally be observed teaching for a total of at least one hour, spread over two or more occasions.

36. Observers should have a clear understanding of the context in which an observed lesson is given. They will need to ensure that they are fully briefed by the appraisee before observation begins. Observers should also discuss their impressions of the lesson with the appraisee after the observation. They should normally aim to do this within two working days of the observation.

The case for classroom observation as a means of bringing about development has been made on many occasions. Here are just a few extracts:

> ...a view of the climate, rapport, interaction and functioning of the classroom available from no other source
>
> **Evertson and Holley, 1981**

> The one undisputed requirement of good education is good teaching, and performance in the classroom lies at the heart of the teacher's professional skill and of the standard of learning achieved
>
> *Education Observed*, HMI, 1985

> The essence of appraisal should be positive. Appraisal should be about "prizing" and "valuing" what is seen
>
> **Montgomery, 1985**

> Many teachers have found observation useful in itself. The major outcome was that it encouraged (teachers) to reflect more systematically on their teaching and this was professionally a most rewarding experience
>
> **CIE Evaluation Report, 1989**

A number of schools will have already used observation for purposes other than appraisal and will have appreciated the value of classroom observation in its own right. Teaching is far from being a routine activity and no one observation is likely to typify the generality of a teacher's classroom performance. Therefore, within the context of appraisal, classroom observation is only one of a number of data gathering techniques available to us. Yet it features prominently within the Regulations and Circular as being the main means of gathering information in preparation for appraisal.

Classroom observation should be carried out within the same framework of principles as the overall appraisal process. Set out below is a list of additional principles presented by

Suffolk LEA which draws upon the findings of several other writers:

- **the observation must be open and based on the mutual understanding by observer and observed of the context, purposes, procedures, criteria and outcomes of the observation and especially of their potential use in the appraisal process;**
- **both observer and observed should understand, and if necessary clarify, their respective responsibilities for acting upon the conclusions of an observation;**
- **the observation should be action-oriented and should be linked to a professional support and development programme;**
- **it should be fair and equitable and should be seen to be so both in general and by respecting equal opportunities, particularly in relation to gender and race;**
- **it should be reasonably comprehensive, sampling an appropriate range of the teacher's classroom teaching;**
- **it should be valid and hence accurate and comprehensive in assessing teaching quality;**
- **it should strike an appropriate balance between two broad purposes: professional development and LEA management of the teaching force;**
- **it should be acceptable to teachers, heads, governors and LEAs;**
- **it should be practicable and should avoid being too complex, bureaucratic and time-consuming;**
- **it should lead to improvement.**

Suffolk LEA (1987)

However, observation continues to be a source of considerable anxiety for many teachers. Some of this anxiety is brought about by a certain resentment that the autonomy of the teacher is being invaded. Another form of resentment stems from those who believe that observation of colleagues at work in the classroom has always taken place, albeit informally. There is little doubt that, for many unused to regular or systematic observation since their early days in the profession, formalised and structured observation will be a sensitive issue. So, how do you limit apprehension about the classroom observation process? It may be helpful to think in terms of developing a strategy which aims at:

- promoting discussion of teaching issues between teachers, perhaps through carrying out a whole school review or constructing a school development plan;
- encouraging teachers to observe other colleagues, possibly more experienced than themselves;
- encouraging peer observation/feedback on specific and negotiated aspects of teaching (e.g pupil involvement; on/off task behaviour; use of praise; use of question types);
- providing for "dry runs" of classroom observation - i.e. short observations carried out by those who will be involved in the process;
- facilitating a self-observation exercise using audio and/or video recording.

The rate at which schools can progress through these steps will vary according to their state of readiness, but for a school that is not appropriately placed for such an initiative the best advice might be to delay until further developmental work has been carried out.

Observations may, or may not, be carried out by the appraiser. In some schemes, observation may be delegated to peers. In these cases, reports on the scope and outcomes of the observation can be prepared for the appraiser. Some of the advantages and disadvantages of peer as opposed to appraiser observation is set out in Figure 6.2.

Figure 6.2: PEER AND APPRAISER OBSERVATION COMPARED

PEER OBSERVATION	APPRAISER OBSERVATION
• the observer may have substantial expertise in an area which is relevant and helpful to the appraisee • peer observation can be less threatening for the appraisee than observation by a line manager • observation by a peer can result in the appraiser not having a complete picture of the appraisees performance • a peer may not have the status to facilitate the action needed to support the appraisee	• direct contact in this way helps the appraiser become better informed about the appraisee prior to the appraisal discussion • keeps the process more streamlined • appraiser might be seen as threatening • appraiser may not be perceived as an effective practitioner • appraiser may not be perceived to have appropriate or comparable experience

There would seem to be considerable benefit in making the first of the two observations a general focus observation. This will be particularly true in the early days of implementing a school's scheme when teachers are likely to be less clear about what constitutes a specific focus area for observation. A general focus observation will involve the observer in taking a "wide-lensed" view of the teacher's work within the classroom. Such an observation will not only give an all round perspective of the teacher's performance but will also help form the basis of the subsequent specific focus observation.

Classroom observation is likely to be more effective in improving teaching if the focus of the observer is narrowed to certain specific features of a teacher's work in the classroom. A teacher's activities in the classroom are many and varied; if the observer attempts to observe all of these, little is likely to be gained and the result is likely to be some rather superficial observations. Data produced as a result of focused observations is more likely to lead to meaningful changes in working practice than the more global and superficial feedback.

Observation inevitably involves making judgements; these must be made on the basis of agreed criteria and records should, where appropriate, note the observation which led to a particular judgement being made. Without these criteria the observer is in danger of making arbitrary judgements, often looking at lessons in terms of how he/she would have taught them, or in being excessively critical on things recognised to be intrinsic faults. Feedback of descriptive rather than judgemental data is likely to lead to a far more productive process with valuable information provided for discussion between observer and the teacher at the appraisal interview.

Classroom observation appears to work best if set in a cycle of:

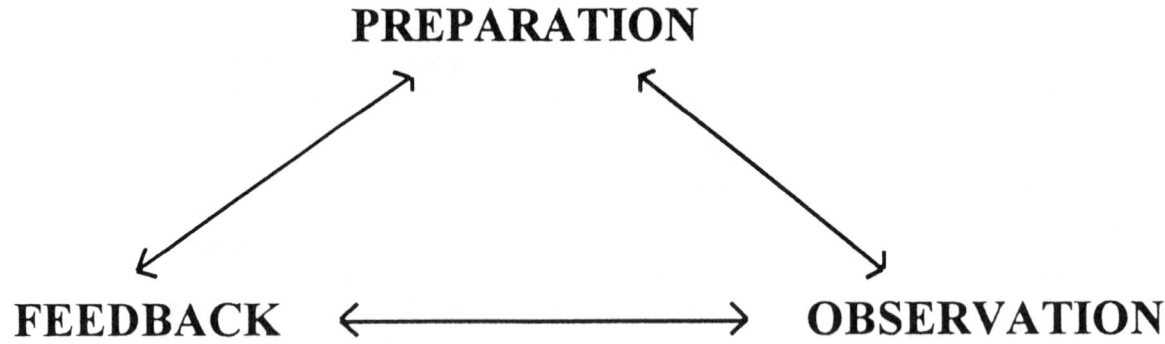

Preparation

At the preparation stage the appraiser and appraisee should meet to agree the time/place of the observation, the focus of the observation and the method(s) to be employed. The style of observation, including the conduct of the observer should also be discussed. Finally, and crucially, the context of the lesson and any constraints will need to be considered.

Observation

There are many ways of observing performance within the classroom. These range from scientific research approaches with behaviour being recorded every few seconds, to more intuitive approaches. It is important that appraisers are aware of the various approaches and the advantages and disadvantages of each method.

The type of classroom observation decided upon will depend on:

- the chosen focus of observation

- the purpose of the observation

- the experience of the observer

The most commonly available methods at the disposal of the appraiser and appraisee are summarised in Figure 6.3 below:

Figure 6.3: METHODS FOR RECORDING CLASSROOM OBSERVATION

PENCIL AND PAPER METHODS	
• Open Recording	observer uses blank sheet of paper and either notes down key points in the lesson, or uses a form of shorthand/longhand and writes quickly to record what happens.
• Tally Systems	observer puts down a tally or tick every time particular events occur against predetermined criteria agreed between appraiser and appraisee e.g. every time a teacher gives praise or asks a closed question. The result is factual rather than judgemental. The aim is to produce a pattern of classroom events.
• Timed Systems	observer scans the classroom at predetermined intervals e.g every 2 minutes, and either writes down what is happening or puts a mark under one of the series of predetermined categories which describe possible classroom events. Again this shows a pattern of events and the record is factual.
• Prompting Questions	observer is asked to provide answers to a series of questions about classroom work. Prompting questions can cast the observer in a judgemental role, encouraging him/her to impose personal views. This can be prevented if the questions are designed to elicit factual and objective answers rather than opinions.
• Diagram	observer records what happens on a diagram of the classroom. This can be factual and descriptive.
AUDIO-VISUAL METHODS • Audio/Audio visual recording methods	these can be used on their own or in conjunction with written methods of recording. They are selective depending on the position of microphones and cameras. They enable the observer and appraisee to replay the lesson during a feedback discussion.

Feedback

The chief aim of gathering data from classroom observation must be to influence the teacher's performance. Discussion of the data by the observer and the teacher during the appraisal interview should lead to valuable lessons being learnt. This will only be true if the atmosphere is positive and supportive and based on the mutual trust established between the two at the preparation stage.

Feedback may be given in a variety of forms, both verbal and non-verbal. In both cases there is an initial need to decide on what precisely is to be observed. Feedback appears to work best if it is:

- given within 48 hours of the observation
- based on careful and systematic recording
- based on data which is factual
- interpreted with reference to known and agreed criteria
- given as part of a two-way discussion
- the basis for future development strategies

In giving feedback on what has been observed the appraiser should:-

- focus on *evidence* which has been recorded rather than on impressions
- focus on *description* rather than judgement
- focus on *sharing* ideas rather than giving evidence
- focus on the *needs of the appraisee* rather than those of the appraiser
- focus on *what the appraisee can use* rather than on what the appraiser might like to give
- focus on *what* is observed rather than *why* something might have happened
- allow the appraisee *time to reflect and comment* to emphasise the dialogue which is taking place
- be *positive*

Successful classroom observation can provide a valuable starting point for the professional discussion on which the appraisal interview is based. However, sufficient time should be allowed for both the appraiser and the appraisee to reflect upon the information gathered and the way in which it may relate to the targets which are set at the appraisal interview.

The following examples are intended to help readers reach decisions about the focus of their classroom observations.

EXAMPLE 30: SUGGESTED AREAS FROM WHICH TO SELECT A FOCUS FOR CLASSROOM OBSERVATION.

PLANNING AND PREPARATION	ORGANISATION OF THE LEARNING
Evidence of planning	*Clarity of lesson/activity*
Relationship to scheme of work	*Suitability of lesson/ activity to age and ability of children*
Work matched to pupils' age and ability	*Relationship of lesson/ activity to previous learning and future intentions*
RELATIONSHIP WITH PUPILS	*Suitability of activities in promoting desired learning outcomes*
Rapport with whole class	*Use of resources*
Rapport with individuals	*Balance of teaching styles and learning experiences*
Teacher characteristics which support the learning	*Pupil pride and involvement in their work*
CLASSROOM TECHNIQUES AND MANAGEMENT	*Marking and assessment procedures*
Organisation of room and resources prior to the lesson/ activity	*Recording procedures*
Clarity of instruction and organised start of lesson/ activity	*THE LEARNING ENVIRONMENT*
Involvement of children and teacher in the lesson/ activity	*Maintenance of an effective working environment*
Organisation and timing of the end of the lesson/ activity	*Purposeful display of pupils work and relevant material*

EXAMPLE 31:   FOCUS: General Focus Observation

PLANNING AND PREPARATION
Evidence of planning   *TARGET*
Relationship to scheme of work   *TARGET*
Work matched to pupils' age and ability   *TARGET*

RELATIONSHIPS
Rapport with whole class
TARGET
Rapport with individuals
TARGET
Teacher characteristics which support the learning
TARGET

CLASSROOM TECHNIQUES AND MANAGEMENT
Organisation of room and resources prior to lesson/activity
TARGET
Clarity of instructions and organised start of lesson/ activity
TARGET
Involvement of children and teacher during the lesson/ activity
TARGET
Organisation and timing of the end of the lesson/activity
TARGET

ORGANISATION OF THE LEARNING

Clarity of lesson/activity

TARGET

Suitability of lesson/activity to age and ability of children

TARGET

Relationship of lesson/activity to previous learning and future intentions

TARGET

Suitability of activities in promoting desired learning outcomes

TARGET

Use of resources

TARGET

Balance of teaching styles and learning experiences

TARGET

Pupil pride and involvement in their work

TARGET

Marking and assessment procedures

TARGET

Recording procedures

TARGET

It is worth remembering that classroom observation is in itself a valuable form of in-service training and professional development.   It takes time to become skilled in observation and feedback and to gain confidence with a variety of approaches and techniques.

Task Observation

Task observation is particularly supportive of colleagues whose role occupies significant managerial responsibilities. For those with clearly defined management roles, an appraisee may request that the appraiser supplement information from classroom observation by observing tasks in other areas of work.

During the pre-interview meeting, therefore, the appraiser and appraisee will need to decide on:

- the nature of the task to be observed
- the method of observation and recording
- the time/place of the observation
- which colleagues need to be approached to gather information
- the questions which colleagues will be asked

The task focus needs to be specific if there is to be quality of observation and of feedback. Anything less is likely to be global and superficial in nature which will do little to support meaningful development.

In deciding which aspect of management should be observed, an appraisee might find it helpful to consider the following questions:

- am I interested in the content or the process of the task?
- am I interested in how I interact with colleagues?
- am I interested in my individual performance?
- am I interested in a strategy or technique?

The focus will decide the nature and extent of the evidence which needs to be collected in order that the ensuing discussion is productive. It will also lead to a consideration of how, when, and by whom the evidence will be collected. The relevant guidance as offered in DfE Circular 12/91 is set out below:

CIRCULAR 12/91: COLLECTION OF INFORMATION FROM OTHER SOURCES
para.
37.   Classroom observation is only one source, albeit a particularly important one, of information. Other sources should also be taken into account, including the work and progress of pupils.

38.   In collecting information about a school teacher's work, including non-teaching duties, appraisers should follow the Code of Practice on information collection at Annex A. The Regulations require the appraiser to consult the appraisee if he or she is going to consult other people to obtain information which is relevant to the appraisal. During such consultation, appraisees should be given the opportunity to express their views about the principle of collecting information from the particular people involved and the method of collection. In the case of head teacher appraisal, it is likely that appraisers will wish to seek information from governors, parents and, in the case of LEA-maintained schools, LEA officers or advisers. Appraisers are unlikely to wish to do likewise in the appraisal of other school teachers, save in special cases such as, perhaps, a teacher with a special responsibility for home-school liaison, although they may well wish to seek information from other teachers at the school.

THE PERIOD OF INFORMATION COLLECTION
39.   The collection of information for appraisals, including classroom observation, should normally be completed within half a term. The information itself may relate, as appropriate, to the whole of the period since the last appraisal and may be obtained through the normal processes of management, as well as through ad hoc collection. The appraisal interview should take place as soon as practicable after the collection of the information. Enough time should be allowed to reflect adequately on the observation. Where a session of observation takes place a long time before the appraisal interview, the observation and the immediate post-observation discussion should be adequately recorded.

A suggested self-review for task observation is shown below:

EXAMPLE 32: TASK OBSERVATION: SELF-REVIEW FORMAT

•   *Consider the non-teaching tasks you carry out regularly as part of your work.*

•   *Which of these is most important in relation to your job?*

•   *When/how often does the task occur?*

•   *How long would it be necessary to observe the task to get a fair view of it?*

•   *Would observing one example of the task be adequate or would a series of observations be needed?*

•   *Would there be any issues of confidentiality or of gaining the agreement of others?*

•   *How would the observer gather evidence?*

•   *How would the evidence be recorded?*

If colleagues are to be asked for information, it is essential that a professional, sensitive and positive approach is adopted. Such interviews should be brief and the appraiser should not allow discussion to go beyond the questions relevant to the agreed focus. Likewise, it is important that questions are phrased in such a way that they do not lead to unprofessional disclosure.

In collecting data from other people it is possible to use questionnaires and/or interviews. For example, a Head of Department posed the following questions to (a) members of her department and (b) the curriculum deputy:

EXAMPLE 33: COLLECTING DATA

1.   How does the management structure of the department allow for democratic discussion and participation in decision-making and forward planning for all members of the team?

2.   How and in what format are the department's discussions and activities recorded and presented to you?

3.   How is your personal contribution to the department recognised, appreciated and documented, particularly the time you spend after school working for the department?

4.   To what extent does the department's forward planning fit in with the requirements of the National Curriculum?

5.   How are the members of the department encouraged to take advantage of opportunities for INSET and professional development?

6.   Does the department come across as being isolated or does it interact well with other curriculum areas?

7.   Are there any points you would like to raise which you feel could help to improve the effective management of the department?

In a recent small-scale research project within my Hereford & Worcester, a group of high school deputy headteachers, in their investigation into peer group appraisal, were concerned with the issue of task observation. They approached the issue of collecting information from others by agreeing:

• who should be approached
• what questions should be asked

The following are examples of the tasks on which their pilot appraisal interviews were based:

EXAMPLE 34: TASK OBSERVATION

FOCUS AREA: Timetabling

WHO SHOULD BE ASKED?

Head of large department; Head of small department; teacher i/c cross-curricular themes

WHAT SHOULD BE ASKED?

What is the process for collecting information about your timetable requirements?
What input do you have into the construction of the timetable?
What are the criteria for allocating time on the timetable?

FOCUS AREA: INSET

WHO SHOULD BE ASKED?

Standard grade teacher; "B" allowance holder; "C" allowance holder; Senior Teachers (D & E allowance holders)

WHAT SHOULD BE ASKED?

What process exists for identifying needs?
What are the criteria for allocating INSET money?
To what extent do Teacher Education Days relate to the identification of needs?

It was decided that no more than three questions were needed under each heading, particularly because of time constraints. Responses were recorded on a sheet of A4, so that they could be compared and set against the appraisee's perspective of the focus area. Questions in this form should avoid personal comments but should provide feedback on the appraisee's performance in the chosen area.

The methods of recording information from task observations are essentially the same as those used in classroom observation. There is no best method, merely a method of best fit. The choice will depend on:

- the focus of the observation
- the role of the appraiser
- the appraiser's experience of observation

Some useful questions to ask at the outset are:

- when and how often is the appraisee involved in the task?
- how long would the appraiser need to observe to be able to comment meaningfully and fairly on the activity?
- would one or a series of observations be necessary?
- would the appraiser need the agreement of others to observe the task?

Figure 6.4: POSSIBLE AREAS OF FOCUS FOR TASK OBSERVATION

Pupil welfare and support	General Management	Specific Management Tasks
• Maintaining individual pupil records • Overview of pupil welfare/progress • Extra-curricular activities • Liaison with pastoral team • Assemblies	• Planning/setting objectives • Maintaining appropriate records/documentation • Organising resources, including human resources • Monitoring and evaluation • Communication • Meetings	• INSET • Professional Development Coordinator • Timetabling • Links with governors • Links with the community/industry/PTA • Marketing

EXAMPLE 35: APPRAISAL OF HEAD OF DEPARTMENT/COORDINATOR OF CROSS-CURRICULAR AREA

Questions asked by an appraiser (Deputy Headteacher):

1a   *Does the department's forward planning fit in with the requirements of the National Curriculum? Do you have any concerns in that area?*

1b   *Are the department's discussions and activities recorded and presented to you in a suitable format and in sufficient detail?*

2   *Do you feel that the management structure of the department allows for democratic discussion and participation in decision-making and forward planning for all members of the team?*

3   *Are members of the department encouraged to take advantage of opportunities for INSET and professional development?*

4a   *Does the department come across as operating in isolation or does it interact well with other curriculum areas?*

4b   *Does the department contribute to the general ethos of the school?*

5   *Are the proposals for strengthening the profile of the (AREA) at the school being advanced at the right pace?*

6   *Are there any particular points you would like to raise which you feel could help to improve the effective management of the department or the coordination of the curriculum area?*

Questions asked by an appraiser (Deputy Headteacher) of a member of the department:

1. Do you feel the management structure of the department allows for democratic discussion and participation in decision-making and forward-planning for all members of the team?

2. Are the departments discussions and activities recorded and presented to you in a suitable format and in sufficient detail?

3. Do you feel that your personal contribution to the department is sufficiently recognised, appreciated and documented? Do you think that the headteacher and the senior management are aware of your work and the time you spend after school working for the department?

4. Do you feel that you are encouraged to take advantage of opportunities for INSET and professional development?

5. Are there any particular points you would like to raise which you feel could help improve the effective management of the department?

Questions asked by an appraiser (Deputy Headteacher) of the Head of Year:

1. Does it seem that ... knows each child in the tutor group well and represents their interests in a professional and caring manner?

2. How do you feel that the needs and problems of the pupils in the tutor group are addressed sympathetically and promptly?

3. To what extent do you consider that ... discharges his administrative duties for the tutor group effectively - e.g. register, reports, etc?

4. Are there any areas which you would particularly like to be remedied or given more attention?

Questions asked by an appraiser (Deputy Headteacher) of the Head of Faculty:

1. In what respect do you feel that the relationship between Art and Technology has become more stable and more positive?

2. Are you happy with the new proposals for Y7 with Art working in Technology.

3. As the National Curriculum is quite heavily structured towards Fine Art & Craft and Art History especially at KS3, do you feel the overlap between the two areas will become less?

4. Are there any ways in which you feel the management structure of the Art department is inhibiting the growth or development of the Technology area of the curriculum?

CHAPTER SEVEN

Components of the Appraisal Cycle (2)

The Appraisal Interview

If the direction in which a man's job is to be developed is dictated by the appraiser, if his goals are set arbitrarily, if criteria are established without reference to what he regards as fair and relevant, if his resources are allocated without consideration to what he regards as necessary...he is likely to be resistant and hostile, or at least apathetic

W.E. Beveridge in *The Interview in Staff Appraisal*

CIRCULAR 12/91: THE APPRAISAL INTERVIEW
para.
40.   The interview should provide an opportunity for genuine dialogue. It should involve:
-        further consideration, if necessary, of the job description;
-        review of the school teacher's work, including successes and areas for development identified since the appraisal;
-        discussion of professional development needs;
-        discussion of career development as appropriate;
-        discussion of the appraisee's role in, and contribution to, the policies and management of the school, and any constraints which the circumstances of the school place on him or her;
-        identification of targets for future action and development;
-        clarification of the points to be included in the appraisal statement.
41.   Appraisal interviews are most likely to be successful when the following conditions are met:
-        both appraiser and appraisee are well informed and well prepared for the interview;
-        discussion takes into account the areas on which information gathering has focused; and
-        the interview is free from interruptions.
42.   Targets for future action should relate to the professional performance, training and development of the school teacher. They should take account of available resources and support and should be designed to help, not inhibit the school teacher. They should be precise, realistic and capable of being monitored. The appraiser and appraisee should aim to agree on the targets to be set. If agreement cannot be reached, the appraiser is able to decide the targets, subject to the entitlement in the Regulations for the appraisee to record comments on the appraisal statement within 20 working days.

At the heart of the appraisal process is the appraisal interview. The term interview is misleading and can easily be confused with other kinds of interviews, such as those dealing with the selection of candidates for posts. In order to reflect more accurately the intention of the appraisal interview it may be wise to refer to it as "professional discussion" or "appraisal discussion". However, because it is the term used in the DfE Regulation and Circular, the author retains the use of the term appraisal interview to avoid confusion.

The interview is a complex process in many ways but, in essence, it should offer an opportunity for the appraiser and appraisee to:

•   **Discuss performance**

- **Discuss career aspirations**

- **Establish targets for action**

It might be helpful to think of the interview as containing the following key elements:

1. Pre-interview or preparatory phase

It is important to remember that much of the success of the appraisal interview depends on the quality of preparation - the creation of a positive climate, the pre-interview meeting between appraiser and appraisee which sets the agenda and the context of the appraisal interview, and the collection of data which has been agreed by both parties. This preparation can be divided into long-term and short-term strategies:

Figure 7.1: PREPARATION STRATEGIES FOR THE APPRAISAL INTERVIEW

LONG-TERM	SHORT-TERM
• Training • Planning & consulting • Self-appraisal • Initial meeting • Data gathering	• Collating data • Agreeing the agenda • Reflecting on the agenda

Preparation for the appraisal meeting should be thorough if appraiser and appraisee are going to have an informed, professional discussion. The pre-appraisal meeting, which should be appraisee-led as far as possible, will need to consider issues such as the:

- data/information to be collected
- means by which the data will be collected
- personnel to be involved
- level of agreement and negotiation by both parties
- general or specific nature of the method by which it will be recorded and whether it will be checked by the appraisee before the interview
- extent to which it will follow the balance of the job description.

The appraisee should come to the meeting:

- having reflected on a possible focus for classroom observation and other professional activities (a self-review exercise is useful preparation)
- willing to discuss frankly and honestly
- prepared to negotiate schedules for recording observations and for collecting information
- prepared to negotiate dates and times for collecting information for the post-classroom observation discussion and for the appraisal interview itself.

The appraiser should come to the meeting:

- having discussed time and venue with the appraisee
- having considered the appraisee's job description
- with a copy of the appraisees time-table
- with a copy of the school's agreed scheme, including some possible areas for discussion of teaching skills and qualities.

The task of the appraiser at the meeting is:

- to listen to the appraisee's suggestions for a possible focus for observation
- to help the appraisee clarify the nature and meaning of the focus
- to encourage the appraisee to decide on how evidence might best be collected to provide the basis for a professional discussion
- to agree the timetable for the collection of evidence
- to agree the agenda for the appraisal interview
- to agree a time and venue for the appraisal interview.

It is important that at the end of this stage both the appraiser and appraisee are agreed as to:

- the timetable
- the procedure
- the observation schedule
- the appraisal interview agenda

It is also important that both feel positive about the shared discussions which they have planned together. Adequate time must therefore be set aside for the meeting if the cycle is to be productive.

Among the main approaches to preparing for the interview are:

- Classroom observation
- Self-appraisal
- Interview preparation form
- Task observation
- Job shadowing
- Selected interviews
- Questionnaires
- Looking at pupils' work
- Analysing test and exam results
- Looking at the teacher's schemes of work

2. Interview phase

During the appraisal interview the appraisee should be encouraged to discuss those aspects of the job which have given him/her most satisfaction as well as those areas which they wish to develop further or in which they feel that they need support. If appropriate, the appraiser should attempt to advise the appraisee on how their strengths and talents might be used within the wider school context, and also what support might be given to develop their professional expertise in other areas. The success of the appraisal interview lies very much with the ability of the appraiser to utilise the potential of the process and bring about a meaningful dialogue. The appraiser's all round skills and preparation are vital to the success of the process.

The interview is likely to have three main stages:

- **Opening and climate-setting**

The early stages of the interview will involve establishing a climate which is relaxed, receptive and, of course, confidential. It is at this stage that the theme of the interview is identified and its scope outlined.

- **Exploration and review**

This is a key feature of the discussion and entails opening up the interview in an attempt to encourage the appraisee to share perceptions about the last twelve months or so. It calls for the use of a range of skills, such as active listening, encouraging, summarising, questioning etc.

- **Setting targets and closure**

Targets, mutually agreed towards the latter part of the interview, should aim to stretch the appraisee professionally. They should, nevertheless, be achievable within an agreed timescale. The school' part in providing adequate support should be considered at this point so that the appraisee leaves the interview with a clear plan of action.

Figure 7.2: FACTORS INFLUENCING THE APPRAISAL INTERVIEW

Factors likely to lead to successful interviews	Factors likely to mitigate against successful interviews
• preparation by both parties involved • clearly agreed agenda • sharing documents • adequate time • appraiser should only carry out one interview in any one day • statement should be written up as soon as possible • good appraiser interpersonal and interviewing skills • nature of previous relationships with the appraisee • all parties giving it high priority • no interruptions	• inadequate time • low priority • sudden changes in planned programme • lack of preparation by either or both parties • not keeping to the agenda • interruptions • poor prior relationships

NSG Evaluation Report

The appraisee should come to the meeting:

- prepared to be honest, frank and positive in the professional discussion

- having prepared for the discussion by reflecting on the agreed scope of the appraisal, the job description, the classroom/task observation record, other supporting information and the agreed agenda

- having thought of possible targets for self-development, and committed to support the mutually agreed targets.

The appraiser should come to the meeting:

- with a positive attitude towards the task

- having prepared for the discussion by reflecting on the agreed scope of the appraisal, the appraisee's job description, the classroom/task observation record, other supporting information and the agreed agenda

- having thought of possible targets for the appraisee's self-development

- having decided how to open the discussion

- having prepared a strategy for structuring the discussion according to the agreed agenda.

The appraiser's task in this meeting is:

- to listen actively to the appraisee's views and suggestions

- to steer the course of the interview through the agreed agenda; encouraging the appraisee to talk constructively about key areas; ensuring that the discussions are positive; keeping the discussion focused on the agreed scope of the appraisal

- to check and record agreement concerning facts and actions; agree and record clearly identified targets; agree and record the ways in which the appraiser is to support the appraisee during the year (this may include agreed approaches to another colleague)

- to arrange a date for the Review Meeting to take place within 12 months of the appraisal interview, bearing in mind the school's scheduled timing of the second year for the particular appraisal concerned

- to complete the Review Meeting schedule and pass this to the school's appraisal coordinator. The appraisee, appraiser and appraisal coordinator will receive confirmation of the Review Meeting date.

It is important that at the end of the Appraisal Interview both the appraisee and appraiser are agreed as to:

- the record of facts, actions, targets and support which is to form the basis of the appraisal statement

- the date and time when the appraisee and appraiser will meet to confirm the appraisal statement

- the date for the review meeting

3.   Post-interview or follow-up phase

Please refer to the sections on "Target-setting" on (p.91) and "Follow-up" (Ch.8).

Appraisal Interviewing Skills

It is worthwhile to consider the skills needed by appraisers and appraisees to conduct a successful appraisal interview:

■   Listening skills:

Being a good listener is an active skill. It involves not only hearing what is being said, but also judging what is meant by the words and gestures used. During appraisal discussions, the appraisee may demonstrate some reluctance to express fear and problems; he/she may be anxious about being criticised or judged. By listening actively, the appraiser shows that he/she is taking an interest, and so is able to help the appraisee to open up. Active listening involves:

- sitting comfortably and trying to relax
- making eye contact with the appraisee
- concentrating hard on what is said
- trying not to interrupt
- not letting personal concerns or biases get in the way of what is being said
- using short nods to show that listening is taking place
- picking up non-verbal communication - facial expressions, body posture, etc
- listening for verbal cues - hesitancy, rapid speech, tone of voice, etc

■   Questioning skills:

Good questioning skills are as essential as good listening skills. It is wise to use different types of questions to encourage the appraisee to give relevant information. Useful types of question are:

- **open questions**

    This type of question stimulates discussion, and encourages the appraisee to give information so that the appraiser can pick up key words and probe for detail. A simple definition of an open question is one to which you cannot answer Yes or No. These usually start with "How", "Which", "What", "Who", and "Where".

Example: *"Which of your targets was hardest to achieve?"*

• **follow-up questions**

These questions enable the appraiser to follow up key words in order to gather more information.

Example: *"If you had to identify the difficulties about achieving that target, what would they be?"*

• **reflective questions**

Reflective questions are those which allow the appraiser to check his/her understanding of what the appraisee has said. They are questions which reflect, or repeat back to the appraisee what has been said. In this way, it is possible to reflect both information and feelings.

Example: *"Can I just check with you that what you did to overcome the major difficulty was...?"*

• **link questions**

This is a useful technique for the appraiser to use when wanting to move on to another topic or checking on a comment or something that was said earlier.

Example: *"If I remember, you said...now you say...perhaps you can explain the difference?"*

• **final question**

Even if the appraisal discussion is completed from the appraisers point of view, the appraisee may still have an issue he/she may want to raise.

Example: *"Is there anything we have not covered, that you would like to raise?"*

In the same way that some styles of questioning are likely to be supportive of the appraisal process, certain other styles of questioning should be avoided for their inhibiting effect on the process. The following category of questions, unlikely to stimulate conversation or encourage an open discussion, are:

• **closed questions**

Closed questions are those which invite "Yes" or "No" responses. They can be used occasionally to check facts, but used too frequently, the conversation begins to take the form of an interrogation.

Example: *"Did you meet the deadline on Y2 reports?"*

- **value questions**

These questions suggest that the appraiser wants a certain answer based on his/her personal values. Such questions put the appraisee in the awkward position of not knowing whether to give his/her own view or the one they feel the appraiser wants to hear.

Example: *"You liked being involved with that project didn't you?"*

- **multiple questions**

Asking more than one question at a time can confuse appraisees because they do not know which one to answer.

Example: *"Why do you think this has happened and how do you think you responded to the criticism?"*

■ **Summarising skills:**

Summarising is important because:

- the appraisee can check that the appraiser has understood what has been said
- it identifies the main points of the earlier discussion
- it can encourage the appraisee to elaborate further on the points summarised
- it helps prevent the appraisal degenerating into a meaningless chat
- it helps the appraiser remember what has been said.

In order to summarise, the appraiser will probably need to make notes. However, this note-taking should not be allowed to distract from the process.

■ **Feedback skills:**

People are motivated when their contribution is recognised and acknowledged, and the giving of praise is the most powerful element of feedback. Constructive feedback can increase self-awareness, offer options and encourages development, so it can be important not only to give it but also to receive it. Feedback then has to be honest, specific and genuine. The following guidelines may be helpful here:

- **start with the positive aspects**

Colleagues are likely to want encouragement and to be told when they are doing something well. It can really help the appraisee as well as the tone of the discussion to hear first about those aspects of the work that have been done well.

- **be specific**

Comments which are too general or superficial are unlikely to be useful to the appraisee when it comes to developing his/her skills.

- **refer to behaviour which can be changed**

It is not likely to be helpful to offer a colleague feedback about something over which they have no choice or influence. For example: "If you were about 4 or 5 inches taller you probably wouldn't have control problems with that class".

- **offer alternatives**

In the case of negative feedback in particular, it is crucial that an appraisee is offered alternative strategies for dealing with the problem. Offering ways in which the person could have done things differently - of turning the negative into a positive approach - is vital.

Example: "*...have you thought of trying...?*" "*...might it be worthwhile...?*"

- **be descriptive rather than evaluative**

Telling a colleague what has been observed or heard and the effect that the action has had is likely to be of more benefit than merely saying that something was "good", "bad" or "O.K".

■ **Giving criticism**

To bring about an improvement in performance it will be necessary, at times, to offer constructive criticism. The important thing for the appraiser is to do so without causing distress or resentment. The following guidelines may be helpful to the appraiser in particular:

- introduce the issue directly
- state the problem specifically
- quote examples
- invite an explanation
- encourage the appraisee to find solutions to the problem
- state the agreed solution
- offer clear support to enable the appraisee to act on the agreed solution.

For those on the receiving end of feedback it may be useful to consider the following points:

- **listen to the feedback rather than immediately rejecting or arguing with it**

Feedback can be uncomfortable, particularly when not expected; and yet it is feedback conveyed sincerely and genuinely that has the greatest potential for bringing about improvements. Before dismissing such feedback it is important to remember that the perceptions that others have of our behaviour can be useful to us.

- **be clear about what is being said**

It is easy to jump to conclusions or to become immediately defensive when being given feedback. Make sure that the feedback is understood before any response is given. A useful way of dealing with this is to check for understanding by paraphrasing or repeating the criticism.

• **check it out with others rather than relying on only one source**

A second opinion might in fact tell you the extent to which a particular view is held by others. An isolated opinion may help you keep the feedback in perspective.

Figure 7.3: SUMMARY OF THE APPRAISAL INTERVIEWING PROCESS

GUIDELINES	CONSIDERATIONS
Ensure that the necessary data is available	To substantiate discussion and keep it factual, all documentation/data or back-up information should be readily available for the interview.
Put the other person at ease	Both parties should try to be relaxed, open minded, aware of the purpose of the meeting, committed to its purpose and be prepared to discuss things calmly and frankly.
Control pace and direction of interview	Both parties have a part to play to control and influence the pace and direction of the interview to keep it relevant, helpful and work-oriented.
Listen...Listen...Listen	The most difficult part of the interview is for both parties to really listen to each other. Listening is more than not speaking, it is emptying the mind of preconceived ideas or prejudices. It is being willing to consider another persons point of view and if that view is better than the one previously held, being humble enough to accept it.
Don't be destructively critical	Where possible, people should be encouraged to be self-critical of their own performance and motivated to improve. This approach goes a long way to remove the unnecessary conflict from the meeting.
Review performance systematically	It is important to stick to the facts - facts which can be substantiated - and that's where the relevant back-up information comes in handy.

Target Setting

During the appraisal interview appraisees will discuss those aspects of the job which have gone well and which have given the most satisfaction as well as those areas in which they feel that they need support. The appraiser will have an important role in trying to advise on how the appraisee's strengths and talents might be used within the wider school context and also what support might be given to develop the appraisee's professional expertise in other areas. Both appraisers and appraisees should agree on clearly identified targets.

Some colleagues find the term "target" an unfortunate one. What it means, in effect, is any goal, objective or course of action which it might be appropriate for the appraisee or appraiser to take in an attempt to support the appraisee professionally. Targets, whether individual or school-focused, should be set with the following factors in mind:

• time and resources available

D

- known direction and targets of the school and its departments as defined within the School Development Plan.

Setting achievable targets within the school's resources will be supportive and professionally enhancing. Allowing or pressing for unrealistic targets or targets beyond the scope of the school's resources will result in a frustrating exercise for all concerned. Both the appraiser and the appraisee have a responsibility to make the target-setting discussion as productive as possible. The appraiser, whilst retaining the ultimate responsibility for the final product, should actively involve the appraisee in the discussion. Generally, the final targets should be the outcome of cooperative activity. It is likely that the appraiser will assume a role which is directive or facilitating according to the experience and particular needs of the member of staff involved.

Targets may arise from the discussion based on classroom/task observation or from discussions relating to career development. Targets to meet individual needs as identified through the appraisal process are likely to focus on:

- **personal/professional development**

Example: ***"Gain management experience in the area of leadership and delegation";***

- **curriculum development**

Example: ***"Devise and implement a strategy to use more small-group work in problem-solving tasks";***

- **pupil development**

Example: ***"Develop guidance sheets to help pupils express their thoughts in self-assessment section of pupil profiles";***

- **management development**

Example: ***"Develop abilities concerned with the management of meetings";***

- **school development"**

Example: ***"Review school/departmental/section policy on marking";***

A useful guide to setting out targets is the suggestion that they should be **SMART** (Industrial Society, 1987), - as detailed in Figure 7.4.

Figure 7.4: ESTABLISHING TARGETS

S = Specific

Setting targets requires reflection on the current situation and clarification of what it is hoped to achieve. Targets should be specific and provide criteria for monitoring progress. They should be expressed in terms of active verbs which focus attention on process. e.g. "Undertake an audit which will aid review of the PSE policy" NOT "hold discussions about the PSE provision in the school"

M = Measurable

Targets not only enable progress to be monitored, they also provide criteria which enable us to evaluate the success of our achievement. They are measures of success. e.g. "Increase the percentage of parents attending school reporting evenings" NOT "improve parental support of the school"

A = Achievable

Targets need to be achievable in terms of time and resources, otherwise expectations will not be realised and commitment to future projects will be lost. However, they should be challenging. There is a temptation to set simple targets which do not motivate because they are not demanding.

R = Realistic

Targets should be realistic and within the resources available. The capabilities of individuals should enable progress to be made. If certain skills are lacking, programmes of training may need to be considered before a plan is implemented. e.g. "Reorganise the classroom to aid small-group work" NOT "plan how small group work could be improved"

T = Time-deadlined

Without a time frame, targets provide no real criteria for monitoring progress. Each target should be linked to a short-term, mid-term or long-term reference point which will act as a marker and help to keep the implementation of a plan on course. e.g. "Complete the audit by the end of the Autumn Term" NOT "complete the audit as soon as possible"

Principles of Target Setting

Targets should:

- be stated in clear, unambiguous language
- be few in number (2-4) depending on complexity
- be measurable or observable
- be challenging
- be realistic and attainable

- be job-orientated and related to improved competence
- be related to, and consistent with, the philosophy of the school and the LEA
- include an "action plan" with steps for implementation
- include some statement of what is considered to be an acceptable performance
- be discussed at agreed intervals during the year by the parties concerned and modified if necessary
- be monitored.

Following the setting of targets and prior to the Review Meeting, the appraiser has the important task of supporting the professional self-development of the appraisee. Asking informally about progress and discussing issues as they arise are just two ways in which this may be achieved. The appraiser and appraisee may also agree to approach another colleague for support and advice in relation to any of the targets.

The target-setting process cannot take place in isolation. It must harmonise with the broader school development planning process. In this way the involvement of staff is encouraged through their identification of individual professional needs and their contribution to wider development planning. School development planning endeavours to blend school, department and individual needs, and maintaining a realistic approach when setting targets will greatly help whole-school planning.

ACTIVITY 11: TARGET-SETTING

Check the validity of your target(s) or the ones offered in Example 35 below by asking the following questions:

1. Is it an end-result or an activity?

2. Is it measurable?

3. Is it observable?

4. Is there a time limit?

5. Does the individual committed to the target control the variables involved and to what degree?

6. Is it sufficiently challenging and yet feasible?

7. Is it in line with school, department, LEA targets?

8. Is it drawn up bearing in mind external and internal constraints?

9. Is it clear that appraiser and appraisee anticipate the same results?

10. Will the teacher establishing the target be personally committed to it?

11. Does its priority justify the time commitment necessary for its attainment?

The following examples offer a range of professional targets and illustrate the action plans for their achievement.

EXAMPLE 36: TARGETS FOR PROFESSIONAL SELF-DEVELOPMENT

TARGET: *Develop a department resource of differentiated worksheets*

ACTION PLAN: *Discuss with Head of Department by (specify date)*
                   Discuss at department meeting (specify date)
                   Collate range of worksheets from colleagues by (specify date)
                   Produce and circulate catalogue index by (specify date)
                   Update catalogue periodically
                   Review contents of catalogue and usefulness to colleagues (specify date)

TARGET:	*Make greater use of group work in teaching GCSE syllabus*
ACTION PLAN:	*Look through scheme of work to identify appropriate topics for group work by (specify date)* *Plan to use group work with both GCSE groups at least once each half-term (first half-term being ...)* *Discuss pros and cons of such work with pupils (end of third and sixth sessions)* *Review value of group work in terms of pupil enjoyment, motivation and understanding (end of third and sixth sessions)*
TARGET:	*Increase use of computer network by groups in years 7 & 8*
ACTION PLAN:	*Discuss possible use of computer software in context of Y7 & 8 syllabus with I.T Coordinator by (specify date)* *Discuss outcomes of discussions with I.T. Coordinator with HOD and department by (specify date)* *Agree specific curriculum development target with HOD and department by (specify date)* *Negotiate training in use of selected software with Professional Development Coordinator by (specify date) and trial scheme of work by (specify date)* *Discuss scheme of work developed with HOD and agree time for department training and implementation by (specify date)* *Review success of development in terms of pupil interest and understanding and the reaction and comments of department staff by (specify date)*

The professional needs of a teacher, as identified through the appraisal process, may be met in a variety of ways:

- through modification of the timetable
- by a change of class/role
- through additional experience in a specific area
- through professional reading
- by job rotation
- through job exchange
- through direct help from colleagues within the school
- through direct help from support staff within the LEA
- by means of focused INSET
- through planned visits to other schools
- through action research.

Between the setting of targets and the review, the appraiser should support the professional development of the appraisee. Asking about progress and discussing issues which arise are two ways in which this support may be given. This process is likely to be informal but is essential if the professional dialogue is to continue through the cycle.

EXAMPLE 37: PERSONAL IMPROVEMENT OBJECTIVES

Please note under the following headings your objectives with some indication as to when you think these objectives may be realised.

AREAS OF RESPONSIBILITY e.g.	PERSONAL IMPROVEMENT OBJECTIVE(S)	TO BE ACHIEVED BY
THE COMMUNITY		
THE CURRICULUM		
LEA & GOVERNORS		
MONITORING & EVALUATION		
PUPILS		
RESOURCES		
STAFF		
OTHERS		

98

EXAMPLE 38: PERSONAL ACTION PLAN
INITIATIVES:
1.   *ACTIONS BY ME:*
2.   *ACTIONS BY MY COLLEGE/SCHOOL/LEA/OTHER ON MY RECOMMENDATION*
3.   *STRATEGIES TO BE USED IN FURTHERANCE OF INITIATIVES (1) & (2)*
4.   *LIAISON TO BE STRENGTHENED WITH:*
5.   *STRATEGIES TO BE USED IN FURTHERANCE OF (4)*
6   *OTHER TARGETS/INTENTIONS*

7   *SUPPORT NETWORKS TO BE USED*
8   *CONTINUING PROFESSIONAL DEVELOPMENT TO BE ARRANGED FOR ME: FOR COLLEAGUES*
9   *DETAILED TIMETABLE* *ACTION TO BE TAKEN BY THE END OF THE MONTH*
BY THE END OF THE TERM
BY THE END OF THE ACADEMIC YEAR
10   *NAME OF THE APPRAISER WHO IS PREPARED TO ASSIST ME IN (A) PREPARATION AND (B) IMPLEMENTATION OF THE ACTION PLAN:* *NAME(S)*
Signed: *Date:*

```
FIGURE 7.5:  SUMMARY OF THE COMPONENTS OF THE APPRAISAL CYCLE




                        INITIAL MEETING BETWEEN
                      APPRAISER(S) AND APPRAISEE




                       APPRAISEE SELF-APPRAISAL
                  CLASSROOM/TASK OBSERVATION(S)
                       COLLECTION OF OTHER DATA




                         APPRAISAL INTERVIEW
                           TARGETS SETTING
                   APPRAISAL STATEMENT PRODUCED




                 FOLLOW-UP DISCUSSIONS BETWEEN
                    APPRAISER(S) AND APPRAISEE
              PROFESSIONAL DEVELOPMENT ACTIVITIES




                       FORMAL REVIEW MEETING
                 ADDITIONS TO APPRAISAL STATEMENTS
                 FOLLOW-UP SUPPORT AND PROFESSIONAL
                            DEVELOPMENT
```

The following chapter goes on to consider in detail the nature of the appraisal statement, its intended audience and the follow-up review to be carried out in year two of the cycle.

CHAPTER EIGHT

The Appraisal Statement and the Follow-Up Review

The Appraisal Statement

CIRCULAR 12/91: APPRAISAL STATEMENTS: TEACHERS
para.

52. Appraisees are entitled to record their own comments on the appraisal: any such comments should form part of the appraisal statement and should be recorded within 20 working days. Subject to any such comments, it is recommended that the statement form should invite both the appraiser(s) and the appraisee to indicate that they are content with the statement.

53. The Regulations provide for targets for action set at the appraisal interview to be recorded in a separate annex from the record of discussion at the appraisal interview: together the two will form the appraisal statement. The appraiser and appraisee should have their own copies of the appraisal statement.

54. The targets for professional development and training should, where appropriate, be separately forwarded to those responsible for planning training and development at school and (in the case of LEA maintained schools) LEA and, where appropriate, Diocesan level.

55. All those with access to appraisal statements should treat them as confidential. The Regulations specify who is entitled to access to the whole or part of the appraisal statement. Beyond this, statements should not be disclosed to any person or body without the consent of the appraisee save in very exceptional circumstances, such as where the statement is relevant and necessary for the fair disposal of legal proceedings or for a police investigation. Legal proceedings means only a Court or Tribunal.

The appraisal interview will have ended with the appraiser and appraisee arranging a date to confirm the agreed statement. After the interview, the appraiser (usually, but not always) will draft a summary of the discussion and a record of the targets set. This account should be written using the notes taken during the interview, and while the memory of the discussion is still clear. This summary should be sent to the appraisee before the agreed date so that the statement may then be amended or clarified before it is signed by both parties. Government regulations specify that this part of the process should take place within 20 working days of the interview.

The appraisee should:

- read the draft statement carefully and clarify any ambiguities

- discuss fully any points of difference and ensure that where there is disagreement, both view points are recorded

- make sure that he/she understand the targets set and the action which must be taken

- take note of the ways in which the appraiser will offer support during the year

- agree a date for a formal review of progress within 6-9 months of the appraisal interview

- be given a copy of the final statement.

The appraiser(s) should:

- send a copy of the draft statement to the appraisee prior to the arranged meeting

- allow sufficient time for discussion, if necessary, at that meeting

- ensure that where there is disagreement both viewpoints are recorded

- be clear about how the appraisee will be helped in achieving the set targets

- arrange that a date is agreed for a review meeting about 6-9 months after the appraisal interview

- ensure that the appraisee is given a copy of the final statement

- ensure that a further copy is retained in school according to the school's arrangements

- ensure that the targets are separately forwarded to the person designated by the school as responsible for staff training and development.

There is often an issue of confidentiality associated with the statement and its destination. One way of safeguarding such confidentiality is to agree that statements be handwritten by the appraiser(s). This can also help save time!

Structure of the Statement

Part 1   Summary of the discussion

This section should provide a brief record of fact and is intended to offer a later point of reference which is jointly agreed between appraiser and appraisee. It might be helpful when writing the summary to:

- base it on notes made during the interview. If summarising is done at the end of each agenda item and then reviewed at the end of the interview, the process of checking and agreeing will limit disagreement at the final stage

- complete it on the day of the interview

- be prepared to go back to the other person to check things that are not clear

- be flexible over suggested modifications as an **agreed** final version is the most likely to receive commitment

Part 2   Appraisee comments

In most cases, both appraiser and appraisee will agree the content of the summaries, and the appraisee will feel that he or she has ensured any points that he/she wishes to make are included. Should perceptions continue to differ or disagreements to persist, however, then this is the space for recording an alternative point of view. Alternatively, it may simply be a case of an appraisee wishing to explain or amplify a point.

Part 3   Record of targets

This section of the Statement should be completed in such a way as to be of use to the appraisee and appraiser in the process of formal and informal review. The appraiser and appraisee will need to agree, and record, which of them is to approach other colleagues for support where this is felt to be appropriate. Any target is likely to carry responsibilities for both appraisee and appraiser. Targets should be as SMART as possible (see page 93).

Part 4   Signatures

Once the statement has been written, checked, modified and agreed, both parties should sign their acceptance. This indicates agreement on what is recorded and a commitment to agreed actions arising.

Apart from identifying professional development needs and the means by which these will be met, the agreed statement may also be used for better informed reference writing. The text of the statement, whole or part, may be included within a reference, but clearly not without the consent of the teacher concerned.

The statement will remain on file within the school until the next appraisal cycle when another statement will be written. The original can then be destroyed.

Examples 39-42 offer a variety of ways in which the appraisal statement may be structured.

104

EXAMPLE 39: PROFORMA TEACHER APPRAISAL STATEMENT (1)

CONFIDENTIAL

ACCESS TO: APPRAISEE, APPRAISER(S), HEADTEACHER, COUNTY EDUCATION OFFICER (Representative)

School: ....

RECORD OF TEACHER APPRAISAL INTERVIEW

To be completed at the conclusion of the Appraisal Interview

Teacher's name: .... **Post held:** ....

Appraiser's name: .... **Post held:** ....

Date of interview: ....

EXAMPLE 40: PROFORMA TEACHER APPRAISAL STATEMENT (2)

STAFF APPRAISAL SCHEME

STRICTLY CONFIDENTIAL

Summary Appraisal Record

(Summary of main points of discussion during Appraisal Interview - including review of last year's objectives, agreed objectives for the year ahead; and any training/development requirements)

Signed: _____ *(Appraiser)*
Date: _____

I confirm that I have read, and agree with, the above summary.

Signed: _____ *(Appraisee)*
Date: _____

Signed: _____ *(Headteacher)*
Date: _____

106

EXAMPLE 41: PROFORMA TEACHER APPRAISAL STATEMENT (3)

STAFF APPRAISAL

STRICTLY CONFIDENTIAL

Personal Action Plan

Agreed Objectives for 199 /9

(List all objectives, with targets, performance measures and agreed sources of information)

Proposals for Training/Development

(Specify any training/development requirements)

Signed: _____ *(Appraiser) Date:* _____

Signed: _____ *(Appraisee) Date:* _____

EXAMPLE 42: PROFORMA TEACHER APPRAISAL STATEMENT (4)

APPRAISAL STATEMENT

Appraisee: _____ *Appraiser:* _____ *Date:* _____

Scope of the Appraisal: the areas considered

Summary of discussion: agreed statement

Date of the Review Meeting:

Additional comments:

Signatures: Appraisee: _____ *Appraiser:* _____ *Date:* _____

E

The Review Meeting

CIRCULAR 12/91: FOLLOW-UP: THE REVIEW MEETING

para.

58. Both the appraisee and the appraiser(s) have a role in follow-up. The appraiser(s) should assist the appraisee to achieve targets, either by way of advice or other means. Systems should be in place to assist the appraiser(s) in this role.

59. The review meeting should take place in the second year of the programme (but not too close to the next appraisal interview). Its purposes should be:
   - to review the progress of the appraisee and/or the school in meeting targets set at the appraisal interview;
   - to consider whether those targets are still appropriate;
   - to consider, where appropriate, the usefulness to date and potential future use of any training undertaken since the appraisal;
   - to provide an opportunity for the appraisee to raise any particular issues relating to his or her work;
   - to consider the career development needs of the appraisee.

   The appraiser and appraisee should record, on all copies of the appraisal statement, the fact that the meeting has taken place, any modifications to professional targets which have been decided and the reasons for those modifications. Appraising bodies may wish to include other sorts of follow-up in their appraisal programmes.

The second year of the appraisal cycle carries further responsibilities for both appraiser and appraisee. Appraisal is a systematic and continuous process and if the process is to lead to development then a carefully managed follow-up review programme is important.

The Review Meeting provides a formal opportunity for both appraiser and appraisee to discuss progress and prepare for the next stage of the appraisal process. No separate written statement is required after this meeting but the appraiser and appraisee should record on the Appraisal Statement the fact that the meeting has taken place. Any modifications to the professional development targets which have been agreed should also be recorded. The Review Meeting may set the agenda for the Initial Meeting of the next cycle. The appraisee will have time for reflection and self-review which will lead naturally into the next phase of appraisal.

The appraiser should:

- support the appraisee in reaching the targets set at the appraisal interview

- ensure that the identified training needs of the appraisee have been passed on to the appropriate person

- plan to talk informally to the appraisee once a month to check on progress

- be prepared to set aside additional time for discussions if the appraisee requests it

- be prepared to suggest alternative ways of reaching the targets if the agreed strategy is not working.

The appraisee should be prepared:

- to discuss progress honestly with the appraiser

- to ask for support

- to give extra time for discussions.

The possible outcomes of the process for the teacher could be numerous and varied in meeting the professional development needs of the individual. Some outcomes will be able to be met by the teacher with little or no assistance from others, but other outcomes are likely to require the aid of the school and its staff. In particular cases, the provision will need to be made by the LEA or the governing body. The identified professional development needs of a teacher could include:

- modification of timetable
- modification to class/role
- additional experience in a specific area
- professional reading
- job rotation
- job shadowing
- change of responsibility related to an incentive allowance
- job exchange
- direct help from a colleague within the school
- help from a colleague within the advisory/inspectoral service
- visit(s) to other schools
- trying a new form of teaching style or class organisation
- INSET in a variety of forms.

The process of implementing appraisal needs to be regularly monitored and evaluated during the months which follow. Without regular evaluation and subsequent monitoring, the process is likely to lack rigour and improvement. Not only will this be very wasteful of the time and effort invested in the process thus far; it will also lead to disenchantment and a reluctance to participate in further appraisal activity.

The most effective way of ensuring success, is to establish a timetable for review which involves all staff in the evaluation process. The following chapter looks in detail at a monitoring and evaluation strategy for appraisal.

CHAPTER NINE

Managerial Implications

Appraisal brings with it a need for sensitive management at the school level. The weight of managing the introduction of appraisal is likely to fall on headteachers, certainly in the first instance, though the job of sustaining the momentum of the initiative is likely to be delegated to an appropriate member of the school's senior management team. This chapter considers the school-focused management function and how it will have to embrace a number of key issues.

■ Links with Discipline, Promotion and Pay

CIRCULAR 12/91: LINKS WITH DISCIPLINARY PROCEDURES

para.

68.   Where a school teacher is performing inadequately, normal day-to-day management will often reveal this. However appraisal may be one, although not the only, opportunity where inadequacies in performance can be discussed with a senior colleague and remedies suggested - whether through guidance, counselling, training or other means. Appraisal should be clearly separate from disciplinary procedures: these separate procedures should be used where the school teacher's continuing employment or any other form of disciplinary offence is at issue. In disciplinary procedures, persons entitled to access to appraisal records may draw on relevant information from them, where appropriate, in line with Regulation 14.

Ineffective teaching, where it exists, should normally be revealed by everyday management. The appraisal process and the ongoing dialogue it engenders could provide an effective remedy, if used supportively. If the teacher's fitness to teach or continuing employment come into question, however, then separate disciplinary or incompetency procedures may be used. Persons entitled to see appraisal records may then draw on relevant information from them in making their reports or recommendations.

The necessary separation between appraisal, disciplinary procedures and possible appeals means that governors must be careful not to compromise their impartiality.

CIRCULAR 12/91: LINKS WITH PAY

para.

70.   There will be no direct or automatic link between appraisal and promotion or additions to salary. But it is legitimate and desirable for head teachers to take into account information from appraisal, along with other relevant information, in advising governors on decisions on promotions and pay. The same principle applies to advice CEOs offer for schools without delegated budgets.

The appraisal regulations are clear that there should be no direct or automatic link with pay and that the new appraisal arrangements should remain exclusively for professional development purposes.

However, at the time of writing the precise relationship between appraisal and pay remains unresolved. In their second report published in February 1993, the *School Teachers' Review Body* have again deliberated on how the pay of teachers might be more closely related to their performance. They make the following observations:

- Teachers continue to be wary about the possible implications of relating pay more closely to performance. Their reservations relate to issues such as how performance might be measured and how equity of treatment within and across schools can be ensured.

- Both the private and public sector have adapted performance-related pay (PRP) arrangements to fit their particular circumstances including their appraisal schemes.

- Crucial questions remain unanswered regarding the advantages or otherwise of school-based approaches over individual-based approaches.

- The introduction of performance-related pay will have implications for:

    - teacher appraisal

    "we believe that it would be quite wrong for the new appraisal arrangements to be diverted from their prime function of assisting teachers' professional development; but, while serving that purpose, appraisal will also inevitably help inform assessments of teachers' performance which school managements may need to make for other purposes.!" (para. 144)

    - the reliability of performance indicators

    "we recognise that the considerable variation in schools' intakes puts a premium on the use for comparative purposes of performance indicators which measure value-added; but we do not accept that any meaningful comparisons of schools' performance must await the full development of such indicators." (para.144)

    - additional funding

    "we are convinced, on the basis of experience in industry and commerce, that the effective introduction of PRP requires the initial investment of additional resources". (para.144)

- Pilot studies and related development work are needed to enable an evaluation of a range of possible options in terms of approaches, criteria and operational factors, as well as in a range of school environments.

    "to examine how the contribution of individual teachers might be assessed without subverting the purpose of the appraisal arrangements." (para.145)

■ Criteria

CIRCULAR 12/91: CRITERIA

para.

60.   The circumstances in which school teachers work and the range of responsibilities they exercise vary considerably. Appraisal should be set clearly within the context of the professional duties as set out in the School Teachers' Pay and Conditions Document, the appraisee's own work and job description. It should not be designed to provide a simplified account of the appraisee's performance against a set of fixed criteria of good practice.

61.   However, as noted in paragraph 11 above, appraisal should take account of the policies of the school and the school development plan. In addition, if it is to be effective appraisal must be conducted against the background of a broad common understanding of what is expected of school teachers and headteachers. LEAs and the governing bodies of grant-maintained schools should set out clearly for appraisers and appraisees the criteria against which performance in teaching and management should be considered. In doing so they should take account of national and, in the case of LEA maintained schools, local policies for education, including the National Curriculum, the publications of HMI relating to good teaching, and, where appropriate, the work of teacher training institutions. LEAs should consult Dioceses about the criteria for the appraisal of teachers at voluntary aided schools of their denomination.

62.   The governing bodies of aided schools may wish to supplement LEA guidance with their own guidance relating to the curricular and other aims of their schools; other LEA maintained schools should also be given this opportunity. All guidance should be prepared in consultation with school teachers.

The issue of criteria is one which looms large within the context of appraisal. It is an issue which concerns the basis on which judgements of good practice are made or objectives are judged to have been met. Rather than tackling the issue of criteria at the end of the process - almost as an afterthought - there is considerable merit in considering it as part of the planning process. Establishing and sharing criteria at an early stage in the process, particularly as a collaborative activity involving all staff, does much to create a climate which is conducive to the appraisal process.

Criteria can be arrived at through a variety of means but a good starting point is the practice of the institution and combined experience and expertise of the staff. Teachers within the school will first need to agree on what counts as good teaching and then focus on a series of aspects of classroom life to consider during observation. The purpose of the exercise must be to find factual evidence to illustrate the presence of desirable teaching qualities. For example, if two teachers agree that "control of class" is an important characteristic of good teaching, they will need to agree also what they mean by the phrase. They will then need to identify what they will look for in a lesson as evidence of "control".   The type of evidence to be gathered might include level of noise, teacher approaches to control, level of pupil involvement and completion of tasks set.

In addition to this type of discussion, other methods for formulating criteria for observation are available in the form of school based review and school development plans. Schools, by carrying out a review or audit of their processes and procedures in the light of their own external demands can arrive at goals and priorities. These can be achieved both individually and collectively. They can be supported and monitored at the various points of the appraisal process and evaluated as a part of the review or planning process.

Appraisal, school review and school development plans provide complementary mechanisms for harmonising individual, school, LEA and national needs and targets. This is especially true in the case of appraisal at the interview stage or during the discussions following classroom observation. Here, new targets can be agreed which reflect school as well as individual needs, applied criteria, and monitoring of previously agreed targets.

The activity which follows (**ACTIVITY 12**) can be incorporated into a whole-staff INSET day and could result in agreed criteria for classroom observation. The same structure could then be applied to a range of other targets.

ACTIVITY 12: ESTABLISHING CRITERIA FOR OBSERVATION

1.   Write down up to 10 features of effective teaching (Do not worry too much about the precise number)

2.   In pairs, agree a shared list of up to 10 key features of good teaching (Again do not worry too much about the precise number)

3.   Agree what you would accept as evidence of the presence of these features during classroom observation.

4.   Discuss how to apply these criteria during classroom observation. What forms of observation schedules are needed to record these?

For areas of specific focus, repeat the process but identify 5-10 criteria for use in evaluating the specific aspects of teaching in question.

The two examples below illustrate criteria established for the purpose of judging performance during classroom observation.

EXAMPLE 43: CHARACTERISTICS ASSOCIATED WITH GOOD TEACHING

- *ability to communicate clearly*
- *ability to form relationships with pupils appropriate to the learning task*
- *control of class*
- *variety of approach*
- *good planning*
- *appropriate use of resources*
- *self-critical approach leading to adaptation*
- *degree of pupil involvement*
- *overall purpose of lesson - has useful learning taken place?*
- *sensitivity to individual pupils' needs*

EXAMPLE 44: TOWARDS GOOD TEACHING PRACTICE

- *Well planned and managed lessons that reflect the stated aims and objectives, and scheme of work*
- *Relevant, challenging and interesting lessons that have a clarity of purpose and contain targets for achievement which are understood by pupils across the ability range*
- *A sound and agreed marking and assessment procedure which identifies the criteria upon which pupils' achievement will be judged. The procedure should be clear, positive and encouraging to pupils, manageable for staff and understood by pupils, colleagues and parents*
- *A variety of teaching and learning strategies which make active demands of the pupils whilst allowing opportunities for different outcomes at a variety of levels*
- *Fair and consistent systems of reward and punishment, understood by teachers, pupils, parents and governors*
- *Well organised, attractive and stimulating teaching areas, e.g. relevant and interesting displays which include pupils' work, classrooms free of unwanted clutter and easy access to resources*
- *Setting clearly understood, high levels of expectation to ensure that pupils are punctual, well behaved and attain high standards of work. This will be reflected in the quality of work and examination results (where appropriate)*
- *Pace is maintained by ensuring that:*
  - *(a)   deadlines are met by pupils;*
  - *(b)   pupils are kept on task;*
  - *(c)   low-level or repetitive tasks are avoided;*
  - *(d)   opportunities are sought to challenge all pupils;*
  - *(e)   passive teacher-directed activities, which make few demands, are kept to a minimum*
- *Opportunities to evaluate lessons in relation to intended goals should be sought: ideally this should involve both teachers and pupils*

■ Complaints procedures

The principle of fairness is fundamental to the effectiveness of the appraisal process in meeting its aims. In the large majority of cases where issues are raised about the fairness of the process, these will be resolved through the use of normal communication pathways within the school. Where such issues cannot be resolved in this way, a formal complaints procedure has to be established by the appraising body.

EXAMPLE 45: AN LEA'S FORMAL COMPLAINTS PROCEDURE FOR APPRAISAL

This procedure deals with complaints about the content of an Appraisal Statement. Complaints about the actual process of the appraisal must be referred to the Headteacher as soon as the problem occurs and a written note will be made of the referral and its result. Copies of this note should be held by both the appraiser and appraisee. The appraisal process should be halted until the result of any such complaint is known and noted. Matters relating to the process cannot be dealt with retrospectively, although a written note of complaint may be appended to the statement.

Conciliation

Where the appraiser is not the Headteacher the appraisee should inform his/her Headteacher of the situation, in writing, within 15 working days of receiving the final Appraisal Statement, giving details of those parts of the Appraisal Statement which are causing concern.

The Headteacher will then use his/her best endeavours to resolve the appraisee's concerns by discussing the matter with all appropriate individuals and examining relevant documentation and will conclude this process within 10 working days by issuing a written statement of his/her conclusions.

Where the Headteacher is also the appraiser he/she will ask the County Education Officer to appoint an independent Conciliator.

Review Officer(s)

If the appraisee does not believe that the process of conciliation has resolved his/her complaint he/she may inform the Conciliator, in writing within 10 days of the Conciliator's written statement.

The conciliator will inform the County Education Officer who will appoint a Review Officer from a pool of senior individuals with appropriate educational qualifications and experience. The appraisee will have a right to veto the appointed Review Officer, in which case the County Education Officer will appoint an alternative Review Officer.

Conduct of the Review

Within 10 working days of receiving a complaint the Review Officer(s) will arrange to invite the appraiser and appraisee to attend a meeting to discuss the contents of the Appraisal Statement. The appraisee will be entitled to be accompanied by a friend or professional representative during such a meeting. The appraiser may be accompanied by a professional adviser. The appraiser and appraisee will be invited to give their reasons for including or disputing specific contents of the final Appraisal Statement as appropriate.

Remedies

The Review Officer may:

(a)   order the Appraisal Statement to stand with or without observations of his/her own; or

(b)   with the agreement of the appraiser amend the Appraisal Statement; or

(c)   order that the Appraisal Statement be expunged and order a new appraisal.

In the event of (c) above, all copies of the original Appraisal Statement must be expunged and a new appraiser appointed. The decision of the Review Officer will be final.

■ Role of Governors

Governors are responsible for ensuring that arrangements made for appraisal in their schools comply with the Statutory Regulations and the LEA 's scheme. Governors will discharge their responsibilities in respect of the Statutory Regulation on appraisal by:

- being informed about the LEA's scheme for teacher and headteacher appraisal;

- receiving information from the headteacher about how appraisal is managed in the school;

- receiving assurance from the headteacher that the school's appraisal arrangements are operating properly, and in line with the LEA's scheme;

- receiving regular reports from the headteacher on the progress of appraisal and a summary of the targets for professional development;

- making the necessary financial arrangements to support the process and the outcomes of appraisal;

- acting as a consultee in the appointment of the headteacher's appraisers;

- in the case of voluntary-aided schools, agreeing the appointment of the headteacher's appraisers with the LEA;

- being prepared to support their own headteacher or staff appraisals through their involvement in the process of data gathering if requested by, and with the agreement of, the appraiser and appraisee;

- recognising that headteachers are required by their Pay and Conditions of Service to be available for the appraisal of up to three other headteachers and to support their headteacher's involvement in this.

The chair of governors is entitled to receive a copy of the individual teacher's targets on request. This information is confidential and cannot be shared or discussed with other governors. However, to enable governors to exercise their governance of the school, it may be helpful for all members of the governing body to receive information about teachers' professional development targets on a non-attributable basis through regular headteacher reports. This practice will enable governors to make budget decisions to support the outcomes of appraisal.

The chair of governors has the right to receive in complete confidence, both the headteacher's appraisal statement and development targets.

Other governors are entitled to receive information about the school's arrangements for appraisal and any reports on the progress of appraisal submitted by the headteacher as part of the regular reports to the governing body.

■ Establishing a Positive Tone

Appraisal is an inextricable part of effective management. As such, a school must take into account the conditions which exist for staff development and innovations in general, the expertise at its disposal and the management and organisation skills which it requires to implement a school appraisal policy.

The skill and competence of the headteacher is, of course, a crucial factor, because he/she will influence not only the key activities of classroom observation, report writing and interviewing, but will also set the tone in which appraisal is prepared for and implemented. Another vital task for the head teacher is the way in which he/she relates appraisal to other executive, planning and resource management strategies within the school. Gauging and exploring the performance of teachers needs to be in the context of gauging and exploring the performance of the school as a whole, which clearly includes the way the school is managed.

Structure does not necessarily imply stricture. It is vital that a whole school approach is adopted when decisions are made about the structure of the appraisal process. The key to good management of appraisal lies in taking the existing reference points in the school structure and building upon these. For the school with little experience of self-evaluation, discussion about the components of the appraisal cycle will be developmental. Teachers need to know that:

- each appraiser will follow an agreed process
- each teacher will perform some form of self-evaluation
- job descriptions are available for everyone, are up to date and are agreed
- methods of classroom observation, which reflect good practice in the school, are discussed and agreed
- time for pre-interview and pre-observation discussion and feedback are built in
- the conduct of the appraisal interview and the writing of the resulting statement will be according to an agreed procedure
- support will be given to individuals to help them reach the targets which are set down in the statement.

Overall, the whole purpose should create conditions under which teachers may be involved in a professional discussion within an accepted code of conduct. Teachers in self-evaluating schools will be used to examining evidence from a variety of sources, and therefore will be working in a climate which will accommodate an appraisal structure easily. However, appraisal needs a formality which acknowledges the legal requirements by which it is bound and such formality will not necessarily be found in a self-evaluating school.

There are implications for preparing teachers for the introduction of appraisal. Teachers in self-evaluating schools will, perhaps, not need as much preparation as others, but they need to understand the formality of the structure which is required. Individuals, operating within the context of the school, are the focus of the appraisal, not the school itself.

The processes of school evaluation are similar to those of appraisal. They are not different in kind but may, in some schools, need to be supported by a structure which is agreed by all staff on the basis of the minimum legal requirements. The contextual base of the agreed appraisal structure will decide how elaborate the process will be. Those schools without the experience of self-evaluation may adopt a structure based on the minimum legal requirements; those with experience of self-evaluation, may develop a more elaborate structure based on the good practice already in the school. Whichever structure develops, the loose approach to self-evaluation needs to be married with the tight requirements of the legal process.

■ Resourcing

The resource implications of appraisal are substantial although schools will be assisted by limited Government funding to support appraisal. The Secretary of State has consistently argued that appraisal draws together and formalises good management practices that should already be in existence. In his letter to Chief Education Officers in December 1990 he emphasised this point:

> **"Many of the things which need to be done for appraisal are therefore already being done; appraisal is just a more systematic way of doing them. The only elements of operating costs which the Secretary of State considers it necessary to assist with in the introduction of the system are teacher substitution during observation and the costs of organising appraisal."**

(DES, 1990, para. 8)

Circular 12/91 (para. 15) indicates the extent of the grant made available by the Government nationally to support appraisal. In the financial year 1991/92 £10m was made available, with a further £14m available each year up to 1994/95.

This level of funding undoubtedly restricts the scope of many appraisal schemes. Yet, it is vital not to lose sight of the potential of the process for enhancing the professional development dimension in schools and LEAs. It is necessary to draw up plans based upon carefully thought out priorities, and to consider which elements of the appraisal cycle are going on within the school already.

■ Time

There is a considerable danger that if schools feel that the time pressures brought about by appraisal are excessive, then appraisal will be reduced to a fairly meaningless and superficial exercise. Few would dispute that appraisal, done well, will involve a substantial investment of time. The anxiety seems to stem from the fact that there is so much else in a teacher's existence these days which competes for the same time budget.

In some schools time has already been made in the reviewing and planning process for school development planning, which may provide a useful starting point for the introduction of appraisal. This could be achieved by:

• blocking the timetable

- using directed time
- using examination/testing periods
- adding to the length of the school day
- using lunchtimes
- using work experience time
- using auxiliary help - financed from the school budget, e.g. for examination invigilation, swimming, etc
- using time twice e.g. during departmental reviews or curriculum discussion times.

■ Sustaining the appraisal process

Before any appraisal takes place all those involved must have received appropriate training. It is important that schools take stock of their skills and plan a training programme from their particular starting point. Regular review and development of appraisal skills should be regarded as a responsibility of all staff. Time and resources will need to be set aside to meet future training needs as they are identified. Training will need to be a continuing feature of the appraisal development of teachers.

Schools will need to identify their training needs at any given time and distinguish those needs which can be met from within the school and those requiring external support. Training for the key appraisal skills of listening, observing, negotiating, statement writing, target setting and reviewing will need to be available in a range of forms which meet the needs of individuals at any given time.

The second aspect of training concerns the professional development which may arise from the outcomes of appraisal, rather than the process itself. The credibility of the appraisal process as well as its benefits for staff will be gauged by the way in which decisions about INSET priorities are informed by the needs identified via the process. Staff will want to be reassured that the information gathered via appraisal will be acted upon. Analysing this information and identifying common needs, whilst respecting the confidentiality of the process, will be an important managerial issue particularly as the school's development coordinator attempts to harmonise individual and institutional needs via the school development plan.

■ Appraisal Coordinator

Schools have found great value in appointing a Co-ordinator for the implementation and management of the school's appraisal scheme. This person is likely to be a member of the school's management team, but he/she will have relevant skills and experience of staff development and more importantly, the confidence of teachers within the school. It may be sensible not to make the Co-ordinator an appraiser so that he/she retains a neutral position in the process and is able to take on the following responsibilities:

- supporting and ensuring that appropriate training is given to appraisers
- supporting and ensuring training for appraisees
- coordinating the timetabling and administration of the appraisal process for each member of staff

- overseeing the completion of the appraisal process for each individual
- supporting the resolution of any disagreement concerning:
  - the allocation of a particular appraiser to an appraisee
  - the allocation of a particular appraisee to an appraiser
  - the focus of the appraisal
  - the data collection
  - the appraisal statement

    or any other issue arising during the appraisal process.
- implementing and maintaining procedures which link training and development opportunities with appraisal outcomes
- ensuring cooperation with the headteacher that targets are set within the context of the school development plan, and that the identified targets are met as far as possible via the plan
- establishing a cycle of review and development of the appraisal process in school, and assisting appraisers in reviewing their appraisal work.

Clearly, it is important that time should be made available for a Co-ordinator to discharge these responsibilities.

CHAPTER TEN

Monitoring and Evaluation

CIRCULAR 12/91: MONITORING AND EVALUATION

para.

71.   The Department will be seeking information from LEAs and governing bodies of grant-maintained schools to confirm that the targets for the introduction of appraisal specified in Regulation 6 have been met. Appraising bodies are advised to keep records of progress in the introduction of appraisal with this in view. At school and LEA level, arrangements should be made for monitoring and periodic evaluation of appraisal arrangements, including the extent to which appraisal reflects the principles in relation to equal opportunities set out in paragraphs 17 and 18.

The implementation of appraisal, including the variety of approaches to self-appraisal, classroom observation and target setting, will benefit from a clear monitoring and evaluation strategy. This chapter explores how a school's appraisal programme, and the elements which make up that programme, may be monitored and evaluated in the context of the school's overall plan for its development.

In the context of this chapter the term monitoring refers to those processes involved in the collection of data and information. These can be active and participative processes and may take a range of forms. Evaluation refers to the ordering, prioritising and presentation of data and the forming of judgements about it. Both processes should be continuous and formative. Effective monitoring and evaluation can:

- inform future decision-making
- improve efficiency
- help optimise resources
- identify strengths and weaknesses
- clarify aims, objectives and priorities
- raise the quality of learning and training
- improve the effectiveness of teaching
- support curriculum development
- support professional and personal development
- give feedback to participants and organisers.

A comprehensive view of the efficiency and effectiveness of the process will only be achieved if there is as much emphasis on quality and the impact of appraisal on professional development, as there is on quantitative aspects such as costs, time and general resource utilisation.

The monitoring and evaluation of the appraisal process can be seen as part of a cycle. Having set the aims and objectives of the process, it becomes necessary to monitor its components and activities. The data gathered can then be used to evaluate the effectiveness and efficiency of the process leading to review and any modifications where appropriate. This cycle is a continuous process but, in practice, a systematic approach which follows a planned timetable should be adopted during the two-year appraisal cycle.

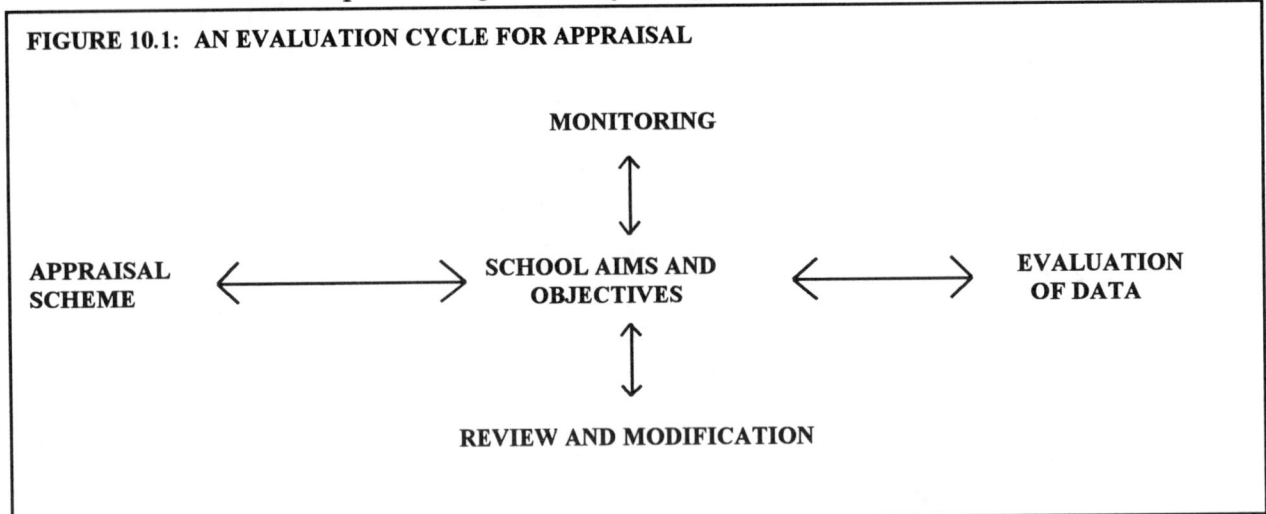

FIGURE 10.1: AN EVALUATION CYCLE FOR APPRAISAL

Why evaluate the school's appraisal process?

- to attempt to gauge the quality of the appraisal initiative
- to gauge whether the appraisal initiative was well designed and therefore effective in terms of its objectives
- to gauge whether the appraisal initiative met the needs to which it was directed
- to gauge whether the appraisal initiative has brought about the intended changes
- to provide a basis on which to become more effective.

For everyone involved in the appraisal process, whether as appraiser or appraisee, the experience will constitute a form of extended training. There should be space for everyone to reflect on the process. The monitoring and evaluation can be carried out by asking staff for their views on the:

- processes involved, e.g. self-appraisal, timetable,4 data collection

- design of the documentation, e.g self-appraisal proforma, agreed statement

- target-setting and support elements.

Such reflection may suggest the need for:

- clarification of purposes/issues

- refinements to the process itself

- further training and support.

Whatever form the evaluation takes, the outcomes should be considered seriously and changes made in the interests of improving the scheme. Appraisal is developmental and it is important at the planning stage to emphasise that the process is not set in stone and that there will be time and space for staff to reflect and to suggest modifications.

The school's appraisal coordinator may find the following programme helpful in keeping check on the progress of staff against the elements of the appraisal cycle:

FIGURE 10.2: PROFORMA FOR RECORDING THE PROGRESS OF STAFF DURING THE APPRAISAL CYCLE

APPRAISEE	APPRAISER	IM	SA	CO	INT	AS	FU

IM=Initial Meeting; SA=Self-Appraisal; CO=Classroom Observation; INT=Appraisal Interview; AS=Appraisal Statement and Target Setting; FU=Follow-up

The evaluation schedules that follow are an attempt to facilitate the process of monitoring and evaluation. They are by no means exhaustive and colleagues are invited to add their own questions/criteria.

EVALUATION SCHEDULE 1: OVERALL MANAGEMENT

☐ Is clear and comprehensive information available to staff about the purpose of appraisal?
☐ Is the governing body aware of its duties under the Regulations?
☐ Are plans in place to provide "awareness-raising" and "training" for all staff?
☐ Does the school's scheme reflect the DfE Regulations and the LEA's Scheme?
☐ Have ground rules for the process been agreed?
☐ Has sufficient regard been given to the Equal Opportunities requirements?
☐ Has the headteacher been appraised?
☐ Are staff aware of the procedures for headteacher appraisal and their possible contribution?
☐ Has each member of staff been provided with a copy of the Code of Practice on the collection of information and the Complaints Procedure?
☐ Is appraisal set within the context of the school development plan?
☐ Has a working group been set up to oversee the implementation of appraisal?
☐ Are job descriptions in place?
☐ Have classroom procedures been discussed and agreed?
☐ Have appraisers been assigned by the headteacher?
☐ Do appraisers have managerial responsibility for the appraisee?
☐ Do any of the appraisers have responsibility for more than four appraisees?
☐ Does the Professional Development Coordinator have access to relevant targets?
☐ Has secure storage been arranged for appraisal statements?
☐ Is there a system in place for monitoring and evaluating the process in school?
☐ What finances are available from: (a) the LEA (b) the school's own resources to support the process?

EVALUATION SCHEDULE 2: JOB DESCRIPTIONS

Are there job descriptions for all members of staff who are subject to the School Teacher Appraisal Regulations?

Does the job description provide the following information:

☐   the title of the post
☐   the status of the post holder
☐   the place of the post within the overall organisational structure
☐   to whom and for what the post-holder is responsible
☐   for whom and for what the post-holder is responsible
☐   the areas of decision-making delegated to the post-holder
☐   the areas of decision-making which need to be referred to other members of staff by the post-holder
☐   to whom the post-holder relates
☐   the general duties of the post holder
☐   the specific duties of the post-holder
☐   the means by which the performance of the post-holder is to be monitored
☐   the criteria by which that performance is to be monitored.

EVALUATION SCHEDULE 3: INITIAL MEETING

☐   Were the practical arrangements for setting up the meeting - venue, date, time, tea/coffee, seating - satisfactory?
☐   Was adequate time set aside for this meeting?
☐   Was the purpose of the meeting clear?
☐   Was the tone of the meeting reassuring and supportive?

Did the meeting help:

☐   to establish a shared understanding of the nature and purpose of the appraisal process?
☐   in the planning of the elements of the process?
☐   to discuss and agree a focus for the classroom observation?
☐   to agree sources and procedures for the collection of other data?
☐   to formulate an agenda for the appraisal discussion?

☐   Was there agreement on the timetable for the rest of the process?

EVALUATION SCHEDULE 4: DATA COLLECTION

☐   Is the Code of Practice for the collection of data clearly understood?
☐   Has the appraisee been adequately consulted before gathering information?
☐   Have the methods for data collection been agreed?
☐   Has sufficient time been set aside for this task?
☐   Is the focus for which data is being collected clearly stated?
☐   Has agreement been reached on the potential sources of the information?
☐   Has agreement been reached on the precise questions to be asked?
☐   Has agreement been reached on the methods for recording information?
☐   Are the ground rules for confidentiality clear?
☐   When and where will the information be gathered?

EVALUATION SCHEDULE 5: CLASSROOM OBSERVATION

☐ Was the nature and purpose of the observation clear?
☐ Was the focus of the observation clear?
☐ Were the criteria for the observation clearly stated?
☐ Was the method of recording the observation appropriate?
☐ Was the context of the lesson made clear?
☐ Has appropriate time been set aside for the observation?
☐ How did the appraiser conduct him/herself in the lesson?
☐ How and when was feedback provided for the appraisee?
☐ Was the feedback prompt, helpful and constructive?

EVALUATION SCHEDULE 6: THE APPRAISAL INTERVIEW

☐ How factual/objective was the discussion?
☐ How relaxed/calm was the discussion?
☐ How could the "climate" of the appraisal discussion be described?
☐ Was there evidence of active listening? How was this conveyed?
☐ How effectively was use made of open questions?
☐ How effectively were periodic summaries of the outcomes of the discussion made?
☐ What techniques were used to probe feelings and attitudes?
☐ In what ways was praise given?
☐ How was criticism given?
☐ What messages were conveyed by body language?
☐ To what extent were the objectives of the discussion successfully met?
☐ What steps did the appraiser take to
  - open up the discussion?
  - keep the discussion going?
  - show interest?
☐ Did the discussion lead to agreed targets? Were these linked to action plans, support, resource requirements, success criteria?
☐ Was there evidence of
  - bias?
  - conflict?
  - defensiveness?
  - blaming others?
  - unrealistic plans?
  If so, how were these handled?

EVALUATION SCHEDULE 7: TARGET SETTING

☐ Has a manageable number of targets been agreed?
☐ Are they achievable in the time available?
☐ Do the agreed targets represent a balance of strengths and weaknesses?
☐ Are they realistic in terms of available resources and support?
☐ What kinds of strategies have been explored to help in meeting the agreed targets - e.g. visits to other schools, change of responsibilities within the school, etc?
☐ Is there an agreed strategy for monitoring the progress made in achieving the targets?
☐ Is the information recorded appropriately in the appraisal statement?

EVALUATION SCHEDULE 8: CONSULTATION

☐   Has there been an opportunity to clarify any misunderstandings concerning the appraisal arrangements?

☐   Has consideration been given to the way in which individual teacher's expectations will integrate with and assist in the preparation of development plans for the whole school?

☐   Have concerns about the confidentiality, access and use of the statement been addressed?

☐   Have the dates for each aspect of the cycle been discussed, agreed and notified where appropriate?

EVALUATION SCHEDULE 9: APPRAISAL STATEMENT

☐   When will the statement be written?

☐   Is there an agreed format for the statement?

☐   Who will write the statement?

☐   What arrangements will be made for consultation between appraiser and appraisee?

☐   Is the statement clearly presented and understood?

☐   Are the circumstances under which the statement may be amended or modified clearly understood?

☐   Are the agreed statements and intended outcomes clearly defined?

☐   Has an opportunity been given to air and resolve conflicting opinions and to remove ambiguous implications and wording?

EVALUATION SCHEDULE 10: FOLLOW-UP MEETING

☐   Has the date, time and venue for the meeting been agreed?

☐   Is the setting for the meeting conducive to its purpose?

☐   Is the agenda for the meeting clear?

☐   Has time been set aside for the follow-up meeting?

☐   Was the meeting helpful in reviewing progress towards the targets?

☐   Are the expectations proving to be realistic?

☐   Are the agreed strategies appropriate and manageable?

☐   Are the amended targets still 'SMART'? (see page 93)

☐   Were the outcomes of the meeting recorded accurately?

☐   Has the appraisal statement been brought up to date?

☐   Are the appropriate parties aware of the next steps?

CHAPTER ELEVEN

Appraisal and the Professional Development of Teachers: Questions and Answers

The Education (School Teacher Appraisal) Regulations 1991 came into force in August 1991, together with DES Circular 12/91, entitled School Teacher Appraisal which gives further details and guidance.

This final chapter offers answers to those questions that, in the author's experience, teachers most often ask about appraisal.

Who has the responsibility for appraisal?

This responsibility lies with LEAs, except for Grant-Maintained Schools where the governing body has this responsibility.

Will I be involved in a consultation process?

LEAs are likely to establish schemes in consultation with all the teacher organisations, the diocesan authorities and consultative groups of headteachers, teachers and officers. The Circular stresses that all arrangements for appraisal should be drawn up in consultation with teachers.

How will the implementation of an appraisal scheme be monitored and evaluated?

LEAs and schools are required regularly to monitor and evaluate their arrangements and keep appropriate records. LEAs may make use of their inspection programme as well as continue to maintain close links with the professional associations, diocesan authorities and other consultation bodies. Schools may also be expected to draw up an implementation plan for appraisal which will support the LEA and the school in monitoring its progress.

Must I be appraised?

Participation in appraisal arrangements is now part of a teacher's professional duties. You are required to participate

> **in arrangements made in accordance with Regulations made under Section 49 of the Education (No2) Act 1986**
>
> *School Teachers' Pay and Conditions Order, 1991*

You are exempt from appraisal if you are:

- an unqualified teacher

- a licensed or articled teacher
- a supply teacher
- a peripatetic or advisory teacher
- on a temporary contract of less than one year
- a part-timer working less than 40% of the hours of a full-time teacher.

What are the aims and purposes of appraisal?

Appraisal is a continuous and systematic process for helping you with your professional development and career planning, and to help ensure that the in-service training you receive matches not only your needs but also the needs of the school. Because it is a positive process, it is intended to raise the quality of what goes on in schools by providing you with better job satisfaction, more appropriate in-service training and better planned career development.

What am I likely to get out of appraisal?

Appraisal will help you:

- recognise your achievements
- identify ways of improving your skills and performance
- identify your potential for career development so that you can be supported, wherever possible, through appropriate in-service training
- overcome difficulties through guidance, counselling and training.

When can I expect my first appraisal interview?

The Regulations state that half the teachers employed by an appraising body on 1.9.91 must have begun the first year of the appraisal cycle by 1.9.92. All teachers must have begun the first year of the appraisal cycle by 1st September 1995.

How frequently will I be appraised?

The appraisal cycle is a continuous period of two years. A new cycle starts as soon as the previous one ends.

Who will be my appraiser? Do I have any choice in this matter?

Headteachers are responsible for the selection of appraisers, and it is possible that if you work in a small school the headteacher could be your appraiser. The Circular recommends that your appraiser should have management responsibility for you. In exceptional circumstances you may wish to request an alternative appraiser. The headteacher has the discretion to arrange this.

What will be appraised?

The full range of professional duties set out in the School Teachers' Pay and Conditions Document including temporary responsibilities. However, it is strongly suggested that appraisal is likely to be more purposeful if it focuses on specific areas. Appraisal should be based on a clearly defined job description which must be agreed before appraisal begins.

What does the appraisal cycle consist of?

The Regulations specify that in the first year of the appraisal cycle there must be:

- classroom observation - on at least two occasions
- an appraisal interview, in which targets for action are established
- the preparation of an appraisal statement.

In the second year there must be a review meeting between your appraiser and yourself in order to:

- review the appraisal statement
- monitor progress in achieving targets
- set revised targets.

The Circular also states that the appraisal process **may** also include an initial meeting between appraiser and appraisee, self-appraisal by the appraisee and, after consultation with the appraisee, collection of data from sources other than classroom observation.

What guidance is there on classroom observation?

The Regulations require that you are observed in the classroom on at least two occasions, and the Circular advises that this observation should last for a total of at least one hour.

What information can be collected about me, apart from the classroom observation? Will I be consulted about the collection of information?

The information which falls into this category is that which is relevant to your job in the school, including your non-teaching duties and the work and progress of pupils.

The Regulations state quite clearly that your appraiser must consult you before asking others - orally or in writing - for information relevant to the appraisal.

What can I expect to take place at the appraisal interview?

The interview is the main component of appraisal since it is the chief means by which your achievements are recognised. It should be a positive experience which offers no surprises and should be an opportunity for genuine dialogue. The Circular states that the interview should involve:

- further consideration, if appropriate, of your job description
- a review of your work, including successes and areas for development
- discussion of your professional development needs
- reflection on your career development, if appropriate
- focusing on your role in, and contribution to, the policies and management of the school, taking account of constraints upon you resulting from the particular circumstances of the school
- identification of targets for future action and development
- clarification of the points to be included in the appraisal statement.

What are professional development targets?

Targets are the objectives you should aim to meet by the end of the appraisal cycle. They should be realistic, precise and formulated in such a way that they can be monitored. They should relate to your professional performance, training and development. Ideally, you and your appraiser will aim to agree on the targets, but if agreement cannot be reached then your appraiser is able to decide them.

Is there a code of practice for appraisal?

An annex to Circular 12/91 entitled *Code of Practice on the Collection of Information* attempts to address some of the delicate issues raised by the collection of information from third parties. This Code is usually incorporated into LEA and school schemes.

Who will prepare the appraisal statement? What will it contain?

Your statement will usually be written by your appraiser **but in consultation with you.** The intention is to record the main points raised in the interview and conclusions reached. Any targets for action will be recorded in a separate annex to the statement, but are still a part of the overall statement. The reason for this arrangement is that targets relating to 2professional development and training may be needed for school and staff development planning. Recorded separately, they can be passed on as appropriate while the statement as a whole remains confidential.

Who will be allowed access to my statement?

Access to your appraisal statement is strictly limited. You and your appraiser will have a copy, but beyond that the Regulations stipulate only that:

- the appraiser should give a copy of the statement to the headteacher
- where the LEA is the appraising body, a copy of the statement should be made available on request to the CEO, or any of his representatives, e.g. Inspectors.

The headteacher can supply the chairperson of the governing body (but not all of the governors) with a copy of the teacher's targets for action, if requested by the chair to do so.

What exactly are the links between appraisal and discipline, pay and promotion?

The Regulations state categorically that 'appraisal procedures shall not form part of any disciplinary or dismissal procedures'. However, they do permit the headteacher or the CEO (or his representative) to draw on relevant information from appraisal statements when taking, or advising others on, decisions about pay, promotion or dismissal.

Will appraisal activities be included in directed time?

Appraisal is now part of your professional duties and should therefore take place in the 1265 hours of directed time.

Do I have the right to complain about the way my appraisal is carried out?

Information on complaints procedures is likely to be available to you, both within your LEA's published scheme and also as part of the arrangements made by the school. If you feel that any aspect of the appraisal process has been unsatisfactory, you should discuss your concerns with your headteacher. Procedures for dealing with complaints about appraisal should be kept quite separate from existing grievance and disciplinary procedures.

What is involved in the formal review meeting?

The purpose of this meeting, which takes place in the second year of the appraisal cycle, is to:

- review your progress and that of the school in meeting targets set at the appraisal interview
- consider whether those targets are still appropriate
- gauge the benefits of any training undertaken since the appraisal
- provide an opportunity for you to raise any issues of particular concern in relation to your work
- consider your career development needs.

What resources are available to support the process?

The funding being provided by central Government is part of the GEST programme, and is earmarked for training and the operational costs of the first cycle of appraisal for all teachers.

Will I have any training? How much? When?

In general, LEAs are committed to supporting their schools through a combination of centrally-run courses and school-based training. Other additional requests for training should be channelled through the school's Professional Development Coordinator.

What specific arrangements are there for the appraisal of deputy headteachers?

If the appraising body so chooses, a deputy headteacher may have two appraisers, which means that technically the headteacher can appoint both appraisers.

Who appraises the headteacher?

Every headteacher will have two appraisers, one of whom should be, or have been, a headteacher of a school in the same phase of education. For schools maintained by the LEA, the LEA appoints both appraisers following consultation with the governing body. The second appraiser should normally be an officer of the LEA.

In a voluntary aided school the governing body and LEA should agree on the appointment of the two appraisers; if they cannot agree, each should appoint one appraiser.

In a grant-maintained school the governing body chooses both appraisers.

Where can I find further information?

Many LEAs have prepared explanatory guidance to support their published scheme based on the Regulations and Circular. You are advised to consult these documents in the first instance and/or raise issues with an appropriate colleague on the staff, usually the Professional Development Coordinator.

It is very much hoped that you will approach appraisal as positively and cooperatively as you can. There are considerable benefits to be gained from an effective appraisal scheme. Implemented conscientiously, appraisal arrangements which meet the wide-ranging aims set out in the Regulations will help to achieve:

- **better management of human resources in schools**
- **more effective professional development and management for teachers**
- **improved education for pupils**

It is important that appraisal now becomes an integral part of school management and of teachers' professional development.

REFERENCES

ACAS (1986), *Report of the Appraisal/Training Working Group.* London: ACAS

Beveridge, W E (1975), *The Interview in Staff Appraisal.* London: Allen and Unwin

Bradley, H (1989), *Report on the Evaluation of School Teacher Appraisal Study.* Cambridge: Cambridge Institute of Education

CIE (1989), *Report on the Evaluation of the School Teacher Appraisal Study.* Cambridge: Cambridge Institute of Education

DES (1983), *Teaching Quality.* London: HMSO

DES (1985), *Quality in Schools: Evaluation and Appraisal.* London: HMSO

DES (1985), *Better Schools.* London: HMSO

DES (1986), *Education (No.2) Act.* London: HMSO

DES (1987), *School Teachers' Pay and Conditions of Employment: The Government's Proposals.* London: HMSO

DES (1989), *Developments in the Appraisal of Teachers,* HMI Report. London: HMSO

DES (1991), *School Teacher Appraisal Circular 12/91 and Regulations.* London: HMSO

DES (1991), *School Teachers' Pay and Conditions Document.* London: HMSO

Evertson, C M & Holley, F M (1981), Classroom observation in J Millman (ed.) ***Handbook of Teacher Evaluation.*** Beverley Hills, California: Sage Publications

Fidler, B and Cooper, R (1988), *Staff Appraisal in Schools and Colleges.* Harlow: Longman

Gane, V (1986), *Secondary Headteacher Appraisal: The Nub of Credibility.* Bristol: NDCSMT

Harvey-Jones, J (1989), *Making it Happen.* London: Fontana

HMI (1985), *Education Observed 3: Good Teachers.* London: DES

HMI (1989), *Developments in the Appraisal of Teachers.* London: DES

134

Hughes, M G (1976), **The professional-as-administrator: the case of the secondary school head**, in Peters, R S (ed.), *The Role of the Head.* London: Routledge and Kegan Paul:

IAC (1990), *Third Report of the Interim Advisory Committee on School Teachers' Pay and Conditions.* London: DES

McCormack, M (1989), *What They Didn't Teach You at the Harvard Business School.* London: Fontana.

Maden, M (1989), in Education 20.10.89.

Morgan, C, Hall, V & Mackay, H (1983), *The Selection of Secondary School Headteachers* (**The POST Report**). Milton Keynes: Open University Press

Montgomery, D (1985), *Teacher Appraisal: a theory and practice for evaluation and enhancement.* Inspection and Advice 21 (1). Studies in Education Ltd.

NSG (1989), *School Teacher Appraisal: a National Framework*, Report of the National Steering Group on the School Teacher Appraisal Pilot Study. London: HMSO

Nicholson, R (1974), The Times Educational Supplement 7.9.84

School Teachers' Review Body (1993), Second Report. London: HMSO

Suffolk LEA (1985), *Those Having Torches.* Suffolk Education Department

Suffolk LEA (1987), *In the Light of Torches.* Suffolk Education Department

Townsend, R (1970), *Up the Organisation.* London: Hodder and Stoughton.

Turner, G & Clift, P (1985), *A First Review and Register of School and College Based Teacher Appraisal Schemes.* Milton Keynes: Open University Press

Warwickshire LEA (1991), *Equal Opportunities Policy.* Warwickshire Education Department.

West, N F (1990), *Planned developmental opportunities - a strategy derived from practice.* Paper given at BEMAS Annual Conference, Reading University

INDEX